Consuelo Leão

Justice

What's the school got to do with it?

ScienciaScripts

Cover image: Provided by the author

This book is a translation from the original published under ISBN 978-3-330-76337-1.

Publisher:
Sciencia Scripts
is a trademark of
Dodo Books Indian Ocean Ltd. and OmniScriptum S.R.L publishing group

120 High Road, East Finchley, London, N2 9ED, United Kingdom
Str. Armeneasca 28/1, office 1, Chisinau MD-2012, Republic of Moldova, Europe
Printed at: see last page
ISBN: 978-620-8-20541-6

To my beloved son Gabriel who, even at such a young age, had the patience of a wise man, and who inspires me every day. To my teachers in life, my parents, Rosinha and Nabor, who have always lovingly believed in me.

ACKNOWLEDGMENTS

To my dear advisor, Claudia Leme Ferreira Davis, who tirelessly attended to my doubts, anxieties and uncertainties, always with words of support, precious guidance and dedication.

To Professor Sdrgio Luna, a benchmark of ethics and excellence in teaching.

My dear teachers Luciene Tognetta and Telma Vinha, who inspired me to continue studying morality.

Professors Luciene Tognetta and Marilda Ribeiro, who gave me detailed and in-depth guidance during my qualifying exam.

Lucia, my director, who has supported me for 10 years and generously gave me the master's degree.

To the teachers, educators and professionals at the Soleil School, who cooperated by sharing their knowledge.

To the director Marcelo Rocha, coordinators, colleagues and students at Lar Meimei, who took a chance on my research and lovingly encouraged me.

To the students surveyed, for the many calls I had about justice, and for their willingness to participate.

To my dear friends Elaine, Rosana, Simone, Renata, Danielle, Alexandre and Felipe, for their friendship, companionship and affectionate listening.

My dear goddaughters, Isabelle and Juliana, my treasures.

To Elita, for her support, encouragement and love over so many years.

To my parents, for their unconditional love and support.

To my brothers, Everton and Michel, who, with their humor and giant arms, never left me alone.

To my son Gabriel, who patiently understood my absences and, by playing beautiful music on the piano, helped me to move on.

"When one person takes a step towards peace, the whole of humanity takes a step towards peace."

Mahatma Gandhi

SUMMARY

The aim of this research was to identify what students aged between 13 and 18 say about the value of "fairness". They all live in a peripheral neighborhood in the south of Sao Paulo and are looking to improve their basic education in order to enter the job market. The nature of the research was qualitative, as it sought to understand the meaning of the concept of justice for a particular social group, through reflection and discussion. The study is justified by the fact that ethics has been put to the test in Brazilian society, so that understanding moral development is becoming increasingly relevant. Data collection used the technique known as a focus group, in which 7 male and female students took part, who were able to talk freely about their conceptions of justice and also express their experiences in this respect. Piaget and Kohlberg's proposals were used to analyze and discuss the data. The results show strong disbelief about justice in the country, as well as indignation about racial or socio-economic discrimination. On the other hand, there was also a desire for the school to teach students values. By listening to the young people, the study revealed an optimistic outlook on the role of the school, as well as the certainty that the treatment of ethics in the school requires urgent and necessary changes.

Keywords: Justice, Ethics, Moral Development.

SUMMARY

1 INTRODUCED

In Brazil, we have witnessed a series of events in the public sphere that have shocked an important part of Brazilian society. In the political sphere, every day we are bombarded with accusations of corruption, embezzlement of public funds, tax fraud and cartels. In terms of the environment, tragedies such as the collapse of a dam in the municipality of Mariana, in the state of Minas Gerais, in November 2015, caused incalculable environmental damage because, due to the volume of waste, in January 2016 the contaminated mud reached the southern coast of the state of Bahia, polluting the waters and damaging the entire ecosystem. In terms of urban violence, there are constant scenes of murders in traffic or the omission of help in hospitals. Such regrettable events also occur in other countries, as evidenced by the terrorist attacks on the Twin Towers (New York, United States, 11/09/2001) or those that recently took place in Paris (France, 13/11/2015). The barbarities committed by the Islamic State and the refusal of several European countries to accept immigrants fleeing fratricidal wars indicate that something in the contemporary world is wrong. But what drives human beings to attack others in the name of their different beliefs and ideas? Can killing or attacking in the name of religious, political or ideological disagreement justify these regrettable events? What are the reasons why individuals think more of themselves than of the common good?

These questions, which lie in the field of ethics, are therefore becoming more important than ever. That's why, it seems, society is making room to discuss them. It's true that these issues have not yet been given due prominence, since they require changes in education that will lead to the transformation of society. But this is a slow process that only happens in the long term. In today's world, there is a prevailing sense of urgency and haste to quickly resolve individual cases of injustice, disrespect, violence, threats, etc. Although this is an understandable situation, academia in particular needs to take a closer look at these phenomena and become aware of the need to research, reflect on and analyze the principles that govern our attitudes and choices. In this way, the formation of moral values such as justice, cooperation and solidarity, which encompass moral development, can make an even greater contribution to guiding the way and proposing solutions that can then spill over into society.

In 2006, while studying for a specialization course on interpersonal relationships and the development of morality, I came across a question that had been confusing my teaching practice until then: was the school involved in transmitting values and building up a subject capable of making autonomous decisions while taking mutual respect into account? I didn't think so, that this was a duty that fell to the family. As a result of the studies carried out during my master's degree, my conception of the social, emotional, political and value-forming role of students has changed. The school is an environment of interpersonal relationships, the best place to discuss values and live them in practice, encouraging the appreciation of others and decentralization away from personal interests can and should be its role. If the school fosters human development, however, it needs to be very careful that it doesn't play the role of judge, judging, condemning, assigning a low value role to anyone. My experiences as a student and then as a teacher, coordinator and vice-principal have helped me to think about the responsibility that the school has in the formation of the individual.

Faced with this conflicting social scenario, and taking into account the importance of education, which in Brazil is suffering from a crisis known worldwide, according to data from the Anisio Teixeira National Institute of Educational Studies and Research (INEP)[1] , possibly due to the low quality of public education, religious institutions and non-governmental organizations (NGOs), among others, have been taking up more space in complementary education and in the training of young people. This research aims to understand and reflect on the responses of students from a non-formal institution, aged between 13 and 18, to problems involving moral values. What do these young people think about moral values and justice? What do they say is the right thing to do when discussing everyday problems linked to family relationships, relationships between peers, teachers, etc.? The space of the non-formal institution plays an important role in the construction of these young people's values, since it also offers, like the formal school, an environment of interpersonal relationships in which conflicts also exist.

According to Piaget (1952/1994), the affective relationship is the engine that drives the individual to act, feel, think, construct new ideas and, based on these, expand their capacity to interact and understand things, because the relationship between affectivity and cognition is inseparable. If affectivity plays an inseparable role in cognition, a prerequisite for the ability to think and judge morally, the construction of values can be understood as a result of what the individual attributes meaning to, what they value and what governs their actions. Psychology has been studying the meanings attributed by individuals to values such as generosity or selfishness, honesty or self-interest, justice, solidarity and many others, which make them act in different ways.

---

1 See *Program for International Student Assessment* - PISA/2012 (INSTITUTO NACIONAL DE ESTUDOS E PESQUISAS EDUCACIONAIS ANISIO TEIXEIA, 2012). Brazil, especially in mathematics, where it scored lowest, obtained unsatisfactory results in the reading and science assessments.

This study is based on Piaget's (1932/1994) research into how children and pre-adolescents understand rules, lying, respect and justice. Piaget (1932/1994), in his only published book on the development of moral judgment - although he had extensive material in conferences and articles - used stories about which children and adolescents gave their opinions, presenting their values on what is right or fair to do based on a problem situation. Influenced by this proposal in relation to cognitive and moral development, Lawrence Kohlberg (1987 apud BIAGGIO, 2006) continued Piaget's studies, creating a scale for the development of moral judgment, also using stories involving moral dilemmas. The answers to these dilemmas resulted in three levels of moral judgment, each with two stages, on an increasing scale, from stage 1 to 6. In the first, pre-conventional morality, obedience to authority and the attempt to avoid punishment guide moral judgment; in the sixth, post-conventional morality, the search is for common welfare, moving away from individualism. The procedure of using dilemmas or stories whose culmination involves an interpersonal conflict encourages reflection and the exchange of opinions, allowing other points of view to be understood:

> It is important that converging and diverging claims, rights and points of view can be identified. There is usually no clearly right or wrong resolution. The situation can be resolved in at least two ways, all of which are acceptable and can be defended equally. The subject tries to resolve it according to their level of moral judgment (VINHA, 2000, p. 468).

The assessment instruments used by Piaget in moral judgment, seeking to identify how children and adolescents think about lying, cheating, etc., and those used by Kohlberg, brought stories to be answered about how to act in certain situations, offering another type of approach compared to the focus group. In the focus group, the participants speak freely and the mediator can use the story as a resource for discussing the proposed topic, which, in this research, investigates conceptions of justice through the exchange of ideas between the participants. Other authors, besides Piaget and Kohlberg, play a central role in the theoretical basis of this research, such as Angela Biaggio and Yves de La Taille.

2 LITERATURE REVIEW

The theoretical framework chosen is based on Piagetian theory. In order to verify what had already been studied in this field, it was decided to review research on ethics and moral values, in order to support the study of what young people think and say about justice. Concepts about mutual respect, heteronomy and moral autonomy, and Piaget's affective and cognitive subject were also part of this research project. The possibility of decentering oneself, of being able to put oneself in the other person's shoes, is an important aspect of life in society, since mutual respect is the basis of a just human coexistence, as the Universal Declaration of Human Rights states:

> Considering that recognition of the inherent dignity of all members of the human family and of their equal and inalienable rights is the foundation of freedom, justice and peace in the world (United Nations, 2009, p. 2).

The philosophical basis to which Piaget refers also makes up this research, as well as the philosophy that preceded those cited by Piaget.

Lind (2000), in discussing the research of Lawrence Kohlberg, an author who revolutionized the scientific study of morality into one of religious or political discourse, highlights the difficulty of studying morality, even though it is a central subject:

> Scientific theory [ë] a broken boat that you patch up in one place and then stabilize, while you repair or overhaul some other part. Sometimes the patch doesn't work and the boat sinks, but not before another boat, to which the scientist can go, moves on. Until a boat moves on, I can express the wish of psychologists interested in morality: to continue the hard work of studying the tough problems of moral development with the tools at hand. (LIND, 2000, p. 424).

Piaget (1932/1994), in his studies on children's moral judgment, points out the cognitive importance of developing moral autonomy. Developing intellectually makes it possible to think outside one's own perspective and to decentralize oneself, but he mentions that these events do not, however, guarantee the construction of an autonomous morality. The author points out that, especially in conformist and gerontocratic societies, childhood mentality remains in adults. For Piaget (1932/1994) and Colby and Kohlberg (1987), morality develops not through moral ideals or good attitudes, since a pre-operational child can recognize a moral value in justice, despite having a limited understanding of this concept. It is to the extent that cognitive conflicts destabilize the child's initial hypotheses that affective aspects drive actions which, combined with the progressive maturity of the cognitive structure, lead to new and more elaborate hypotheses.

The discussion of moral dilemmas is one of the possible paths in education based on Piaget's ideas, since they cause cognitive conflicts that unbalance the subjects and lead them to activate the mechanisms of assimilation and accommodation. Devries and Zan (1998) present the concept of a moral dilemma: it is "a situation in which conflicting claims, rights or points of view can be identified". (p. 179). Colby and Kohlberg (1987) used moral dilemmas in their research, evaluating the participants' responses and their justifications for the solutions given, based on which they postulated stages in the development of moral judgment.

The instrument developed by Colby and Kohlberg (1987), *Moral Judgment Interview,* in their book *The Measurement of Moral Judgment* (volumes 1 and 2), led to research that organized the developmental stages of moral judgment, verifying in it, as Piaget indicated, a gradation. In Brazil, some translations of the instruments used by Kohlberg, especially those that emphasized decision-making and the formulation of moral judgments, have been made, although it is known that these instruments are somewhat ambiguous:

> None of these criteria is an unambiguous sign of morality or immorality. A person who always helps others may not be as moral as they seem. Such a person may have selfish motives, just as a criminal may have acted against an unjust law or a preacher of moral values may in reality be a hypocrite and a brutal murderer may feel no guilt or shame at all (LIND, 2000, p. 424).

While Colby and Kohlberg (1987) analyzed the developmental stages of moral judgment in their studies, Lind's (2000) research attempted to measure moral competence. The study of morality, however, has been accused of indicating only common-sense results and, for this reason, of lacking a scientific foundation. Although this argument should be considered, since the psychology that studies morality uses people's opinions about everyday situations, which are formed in historical and cultural contexts, the same results have been found in different countries. This suggests that the Piagetian theoretical basis has a universal character, which is independent, to a certain extent, of the various scenarios and cultures in which people live, although these do shed light on the understanding of moral decisions. The difference between common sense and psychological science is pointed out by Bock, Furtado and Teixeira (2001):

> When we do science, we base ourselves on everyday reality and think about it. We move away from it in order to reflect and know beyond its appearances. Everyday life and the scientific knowledge we have of reality come closer together and move apart: they come closer together because science refers to reality; they move apart because science abstracts reality in order to understand it better, in other words, science moves away from reality, transforming it into an object of investigation - which enables the construction of scientific knowledge about reality. (p. 16)

Among Brazilian researchers, one author who stands out is Yves de La Taille, who has dedicated himself to studying morality. In 2006, he evaluated the moral values of a sample of young people in Sao Paulo in various aspects: progress in the 21st century, morality, politics, religion, science, art, the judiciary, school, etc., presenting the degree of reliability of the results, their importance and influence on everyday life. Other issues such as the self-assessment of school grades, the reliability of the judiciary, the importance of politicians to society and the influence of the media on values were also addressed.

La Taille (2006) reinforces the importance of searching for academic results that can provide greater knowledge about ethical education in Brazil and the possibilities of expanding and/or transforming it. This interest is based on the education of the new generations, and it is a challenge to achieve the prospect of a "good life" for oneself and for the social group.

In the last five years, instruments have been used to measure levels of moral judgment. Bataglia, Moraes and Lepre (2010) presented instruments created by Lawrence Kohlberg and Colby, such as: *Moral Jugdment test* (MJT), *Moral Jugdment Interview* (MJI) and *Defining Issue Test* (DIT). These tests measure moral judgment and moral competence. Rique et al (2013) tested the MJT in Brazil with young people who, on average, were 19 years old, comparing it to results obtained in research conducted in the 70s and 80s. In addition to an interview, participants were also asked about the meaning of justice, which revealed advanced and primitive conceptions. The answers about justice resulted in five categories, which are briefly presented below:

1. Justice is conceived as a social ethic and an instrument for distinguishing between right and wrong;
2. Justice as law and constitution;
3. Justice as a judgment that brings personal and social balance;
4. Justice as a right and equal guarantees and protections;
5. Disbelief in justice or difficulty in defining it.

When comparing the results, it was found that, in the 1970s and 1980s, young people were predominantly between two stages of the conventional level, with a slight tendency towards the post-conventional level. In the current research, young people showed consolidated moral judgment at the conventional level.

Colby and Kohlberg (1987), with the MJI instrument, established three levels, each with two stages, under which they move from the level of heteronomy towards moral autonomy. These results were built up through interviews and moral dilemmas with children and adolescents, which, based on the answer to the problem and the justification given for the answer, were perceived as fitting into one of the levels.

At level 1, prd-conventional, morality is heteronomous, governed by external rules. In stage 1 of this same level, the orientation is towards punishment and obedience. There is difficulty in considering two points of view and the act is judged wrong if there is a physical consequence, without considering the intention. Authority is defined by the status of power (parents, teacher, principal, boss). In stage 2, the orientation is hedonistic, the right action is considered in terms of pleasure or satisfaction. The expression "an eye for an eye, a tooth for a tooth" guides the reciprocity of this stage.

At conventional level 2, morality is based on laws. Maintaining order is considered important. In stage 3 of this level, the orientation that guides decisions is that of the "good boy". Social approval is valued, i.e. good behavior is that which is approved of by people. Morality is still heteronomous, intent is considered, but putting oneself in the other person's shoes is difficult. In stage 4, the orientation is towards the law and social order. Respect for rules, laws and authority is due to the fulfillment of duty, which maintains social order and prevents chaos in the event of non-compliance.

At level 3, post-conventional, morality is no longer defined by laws, but by universal principles and values. At stage 5, laws are not valid because they are laws; both they and unjust moral customs must be changed for a democratic contract. In stage 6, the individual recognizes universal ethical principles that transcend laws. If a law is unjust, the individual at this stage breaks it, realizing that this is their moral action. Kohlberg gave the example of personalities such as Jesus Christ, Gandhi and Martin Luther King who thought in this stage (BIAGGIO, 2006).

Tavares and Menin (2015) built, tested and validated a scale to assess schoolchildren's and teachers' adherence to socio-moral values. Using problem situations presented to elementary and middle school children and teachers, the authors verified how the participants solved problems involving values such as solidarity, justice, respect and democratic coexistence.

Regarding the value of justice, which is what interests this research, the results of Tavares and Menin (2015) showed that children and adolescents responded to the problem situations primarily by adhering to Level II, where maintaining a good image, or being a good boy or girl in the eyes of others, is what guides action. At this level, respecting the rules established by public or private authorities (police chief, school principal, teachers, parents) is considered the right thing to do. Teachers, on the other hand, primarily adhered to Level III, which is based on equality and obedience to the law. No student or teacher responded in agreement with Level IV, which considers respect for dignity, the presence of respect for duties and the recognition of equal rights for all, under the same conditions, thus opting for dialogue rather than sanction.

3 THEORETICAL FRAMEWORK

3.1 Aristotelian and Kantian moral principles

Moral unworthiness, according to Aristotle, lies in failing to develop one's talents and, in this sense, undermining the universe. Aristotle's writings therefore value the individual, his role and his purpose in the universe. Humanity is not considered from this perspective; man in his natural condition is central. Bearing in mind that considering humanity would imply considering all subjects equal, Aristotle didn't believe that equality took precedence over individual value: the most worthy is the individual to whom talents and/or virtues have been attributed, because they are superior to the rest. Although this hierarchy in terms of the value of man is present in Aristotle's thinking, the theory does not disregard the sense of nationhood, in other words, that of collectivity. In "Etica para Nicomaco" (ARISTOTELES, 2015), the function of the state, politics and science is to serve the community, to act for the common good, an action seen as more beautiful and more worthy than the individual:

> Since politics uses the other sciences and, on the other hand, legislates on what we should and shouldn't do, the purpose of this science must encompass that of the others, so that this purpose will be the human good. In fact, although this end is the same for both the individual and the state, that of the latter seems to be something greater and more complete, both to be achieved and to be preserved. Although it is well worth achieving this end for an individual alone, it is more beautiful and more divine to achieve it for a nation or for city-states (p. 50).

In the book "Nicomachean Ethics", Aristotle presents the idea of justice as something strictly social. Therefore, being just implies being just to someone, just as one can be unjust to someone else. Being the greatest of virtues, justice is "[...] the only virtue that seems to be a good for others, since it concerns others [...]" (MAFFETTONE; VECA, 2005, p. 51). Although the virtuous were seen as different from the rest, as superior due to their natural talents, Aristotle brings up the idea that giving up one's self for the good of others is a virtue. Being able to provide a service to someone who will give you nothing in return, apart from a supposed personal sense of duty (ARISTOTELES, 1984), makes justice a complete virtue, because it can be turned to someone, who can be a loved one, a stranger or a superior, in other words, anyone, not for personal compensation, but considering the greater good of justice. However, for Aristotle, even if giving up personal compensation is an act of justice, acting in this way can also be a type of injustice, if it violates moral precepts. "Let's also consider that if one person commits adultery with a view to gaining an advantage and obtains some profit, another commits adultery suffering loss or damage due to concupiscence." (MAFFETTONE; VECA, 2005, p. 52). Reflecting on Aristotelian injustice, the first seems to be an unjust person who seeks to take advantage, while the other is an intemperate person. Although unjust attitudes are generally the result of vices, there is a partial justice that fits into total justice. Total justice is seen as the rule of law, the fulfillment of legality, the search for fairness. Partial justice, based on vices, can involve breaking the law.

> One, however, refers only to honor, riches or salvation, or all of the above, if we can sum it up in a single term, and has as its objective the pleasure that derives from profit; the other, on the other hand, concerns everything for which the honest man acts (MAFFETTONE; VECA, 2005, p. 52).

On this premise, the vice that leads to unjust action by intemperance is different from that of premeditated advantage, since it has no vice as its referent, only injustice.

Aristotle (1984), when discussing the vision of justice whose principle is the common good, social maintenance, correcting or repairing injustice and iniquity, brings to light distributive justice and corrective justice. Distributive justice, which is based on geometric equality, establishes a third element, which stipulates the criterion of proportionality to decide what is fairest. In corrective justice, the criterion is arithmetic equality, such as 1 notebook for each student, 3 plates of food for all citizens, etc. In distributive justice, the criterion could be 4 plates of food for manual laborers, considering that they need more food because of their physical effort. Both try to bring people's rights closer together by correcting inequalities, something that, in Brazilian universities, could be interpreted by the entry quota for blacks and Indians. In an analogy to Aristotle's corrective justice, everyone should have access to a public university, but there aren't enough places for everyone who finishes high school. In this way, a third element is established, which stipulates merit as a criterion, belonging to distributive justice. Whoever scores the highest, demonstrating greater academic competence, receives a place at university and, if they belong to a historically disadvantaged group, they enter university both on merit for the results achieved and for belonging to less privileged ethnic groups.

In the Bible, Book of Kings, chapter 3, 16-28, a passage about King Solomon tells the story of a criterion of justice. The text tells the story of two prostitutes, both with babies close in age, who lived in the same house. One day, one of them falls asleep on her son and kills him. When she realizes that her son is dead, she switches the babies. The mother of the living child wakes up and sees the dead baby next to her, but she knows it's not her son. When she asks her friend about the baby swap, she tells her that there was no swap and that she has accepted her son's death. Disgruntled, she decides to go to the king so that he can judge who was right. King Solomon asks them to bring a sword and proposes cutting the baby in half, giving one part to each of them. The real mother soon gives up custody of her son, asking the king to keep him alive and for him to be taken care of by the other woman, while the false mother says it's better to cut the child up so that he won't be the property of either one or the other. The king, faced with this, orders that the baby not be killed and gives him to the one who asked for his life.

By establishing corrective justice, solving the problem arithmetically and giving equal shares to each of the mothers, King Solomon establishes a criterion of justice based on equality, which is worth little or nothing. The solution would not be fair in this situation, because killing someone and giving equal shares to each of the claimants would not be fair to the baby's life. However, the king's final decision establishes a third element, a criterion of proportionality, which leads to the mother who would rather lose her child than see it killed being awarded the prize, a situation based on distributive justice.

In his philosophy, Immanuel Kant (1724-1804) dedicated himself, especially in one of his works, the "Critique of Practical Reason", to analyzing issues related to ethics that would transcend time and reach the present day. The concepts developed by Kant are taken up in the works of Jean Piaget and Kohlberg on morality and ethics, although both criticize the Kantian proposal. Ethics has been discussed since antiquity. Kant analyzed the thoughts of the philosopher Aristotle (384 BC - 322 BC), for whom moral dignity derives from the practice of virtues and talents. The premise is that everything in nature has a purpose, because nothing exists without a purpose, everything works for a purpose. From this perspective, the Greek aphorism "know thyself" is in line with this statement, since a man who doesn't know himself or doesn't give himself a function in the cosmos, a purpose, is worthless. Self-knowledge offers the possibility of discovering one's own talents and putting them into practice. Moral dignity is revealed by living well, something that stems from the exercise of talents, in other words, from what man was given at birth, satisfying the law of purpose, of his place in the universe.

Kant's ethics (2015) refutes ancient Greek philosophy, according to which moral dignity is based on man's nature and his natural talents, a perspective based on inequality, i.e. some are naturally more worthy than others. Kant also argues that reason makes man capable of supplanting his nature in favor of ethics. For this author, nature is understood as the expression of man's will, desires and impulses, and it - nature - cannot subdue man. On the contrary:

> The difference between the laws of a nature to which the will is subject and those of a nature that is subject to a will (with a view to what it has to do with free actions) depends on the fact that in the former the objects have to be the causes of the representations that determine the will, while in the latter the cause of the objects must be the will, so that their causality has placed its determining foundation merely in the pure rational faculty, which can therefore also be called pure practical reason. (KANT, 2015, p. 77)

It is man's free rational condition that makes him capable of controlling his impulses and, therefore, his nature, which makes him morally worthy. For Kant (2015), ethics is that of duty, in other words, that which gives man a rational role beyond himself, which seeks the good of humanity:

> Kantian ethics is an ethics of duty, which as such implies a self-coercion of reason, but which also makes duty and freedom internally compatible. Without admitting this compatibility, we fall into heteronomy or the presumption of a moral spontaneity. (ROHDEN, 2015 apud KANT, 2015, p. 11)

Natural talent - or, according to Aristotelian philosophy, that which differentiates man by the dignity (greater or lesser) that it represents in humanity - brings, from this perspective, a hierarchy of nobility, including moral nobility. In the light of this idea, the noblest person is the one who possesses the most natural talents. For Kant, possessing natural talents has nothing to do with morality. It is the decision made by man about how he will use his talent for the common good that is related to morality. According to the author, there is a relationship of natural inequality of talents between men, which differentiates them in terms of the virtues and/or talents they each have. However, there is also a relationship of equality in terms of man's freedom to exercise his reason and his choices. In this way, man is not dependent on nature, but on his freedom of choice.

The concept of equality and universality are present in Kantian ethics: every man is equal in terms of the possibility of dignifying himself morally, based on his own will, when he seeks the good life, in other words, the fulfillment of moral duties. For Kant (2015), the fundamental law of the pure "Critique of Practical Reason" is to act "in such a way that the maxim of your will can always be valid at the same time as the principle of universal legislation." (KANT, 2015, p. 63) and also in the categorical imperative to treat "every human being as an end in himself and not merely as a means." These are values that underline the importance of will and respect, because they affirm that all men deserve them, regardless of their social position or usefulness. Treating human beings as a means of achieving something (associated with work or interpersonal relationships) violates the concept of equality. In the works of Piaget and Kohlberg, equality is evidenced as the possibility of choice, as advocated by Kant. It is also worth noting that cognition is also, for Piaget and Kohlberg, a condition for moral development, something that will only be achieved on the basis of chronological age and cognitive evolution, allowing for autonomy and, with it, conscious freedom of choice.

3.2 Social, affective and cognitive being - Piaget

In order to deal with the question of morality in all its ontological, social, cognitive and affective complexity, it is essential to indicate who the epistemic subject is. For Piaget (1975), the epistemic subject is the subject of knowledge. His studies have contributed to how man constructs knowledge and what the cognitive mechanisms are that structure the development process. Thus, to speak of intelligence in the light of his theory is to speak of mental organizations that allow for a variety of ways to reach the same end. In this sense, both cognitive structure and biological maturation, as well as physical and social experience are central.

The active role of the subject is a premise of this line of theory, since the cognitive structure is developed precisely through the relationships maintained in the physical and social environment, which engender cognitive conflicts that destructure cognition and lead to the search for new mental adaptations that expand the condition to know, experiment and develop. Relationships with the physical environment enable the subject (child or adult) to create and test hypotheses that help them understand things and how they work. Experience is very important for the formulation of ideas which, depending on the stage of development the subject is at, will lead to hypotheses that follow the logic of childhood, progressively moving towards the reflexive logic that is typical of adults. However, this does not mean that cognitive development necessarily takes place at certain chronological ages. Although, according to Piaget, the stages of cognitive development have been presented in a temporal sequence, with approximate ages for the appearance of each stage, this only reveals the potential for comprehension that is approximately compatible with certain ages, and not that development occurs solely on the basis of the individual's biological maturation. Cognitive advances depend on social interaction and physical experience, because it is these aspects that lead to knowledge and the development of intelligence.

> Piaget considers that intelligence - adaptive thought and action - develops in a sequence of age-related stages. [...] In a very real sense, therefore, Piaget's theory takes nature and education into account at the same time (ELKIND, 1978, p. 35).

The subject thinks for him/herself, based on the influence of affective aspects, which are characterized as both emotions and feelings, the group in which he/she is inserted, his/her personal pressures and desires. With this in mind, it is possible to say that children in the pre-operational stage - from approximately two to six years old - have a logic typical of their cognitive potential, capable of understanding the world through their symbolic representations. These representations are presented in such a way as to privilege their need to know and experience the social and physical world, given that their thinking is marked by egocentrism and does not provide the conditions for knowing and experiencing the world to be different from the perspective of the one who has it. According to this childish belief, the child believes that others think like them and that the world is what they believe it to be, like the movement of the moon that follows them or chases them on their way home, even if the rotational movement is explained to them. Egocentrism marks a certain comfort with one's personal beliefs, since one is unconcerned with convincing others of what one thinks.

Piaget (2005, p. 33) states that "logic develops as a function of the socialization of thought". From this perspective, it can be said that egocentrism hinders socialization because, as the author rightly adds, "egocentrism is, in its essence, an indifference between the self and the social environment" (PIAGET, 1932/1994, p. 81). It's worth pointing out that it's not a question of there being no interaction, since this occurs naturally, but rather the impossibility of socialization, since the latter presupposes the understanding that people don't think in the same way. The child lacks the feeling of reciprocity, of seeing the other person as capable of ideas of their own, whether common or different from their own. This is what stands in the way of the real socialization of thought.

Egocentric thinking is a relevant characteristic for moral development, as it marks the inability to put oneself in the other person's shoes. At this stage of thought, the child considers their perspectives to be central and fully understood, as they have difficulty coordinating different points of view. Fortuna (1996) explains that preoperational children focus their attention on a particular aspect of reality and are unable to balance their reasoning with other aspects (VINHA, 2000).

Morality requires presupposed logic/reason in its development. Depending on how children build their knowledge and consequently progress through the stages of cognitive development, there are also advances in moral development. In their moral judgment, pre-operational children suffer because of their cognitive incapacity. Thus, the pre-operative child is heteronomous, considering their duties and values from the perspective of others and not yet for themselves. In this way, intellectual development serves as a foundation for moral development.

Piaget points out that moral development is built on interactions with the environment. In his book "The Moral Judgement of the Child", Piaget analyzes the responses given by children to scenes of conflict, seeking to ascertain what moral judgement they make. Piaget's studies result in hierarchically organized stages, which begin with pre-morality, or the absence of moral awareness, up to moral autonomy, when the subject is capable of simultaneously and equally considering their own needs and those of others.

3.3 Pre-morality

Pre-morality, which lasts from birth to approximately four or five years of age, is characterized by the absence of norms (VINHA, 2000). A small child, aged one or two, for example, is not born knowing that pulling out a pile of ironed clothes and dropping them on the floor can be a joke that annoys the person who worked on it. It's not uncommon for an adult to attribute a certain action to evil, as if the action happened to harm and upset the other person, as if this "moral personality" was already born in the child. On the contrary, Piaget considers that, at this stage, the child begins to learn moral rules and, also, that their actions are not intended to provoke the other, but are the result of their cognitive capacity, marked by the internal need for movement, exploration and experimentation, which disregard the wishes of the other. The absence of norms is called *anomie.* The child needs help from their family or caregiver, in short, from the social environment to know what they can (or can't) do, so that they can then internalize these norms.

The transition from anomie to heteronomy reveals a new understanding, as the child, around the age of two, understands that the rule is governed by the adult and begins to differentiate between right and wrong, although they are not yet able to make decisions that take into account their needs and those of others. Moral feelings are beginning to be built up, such as the feeling of obligation. Pre-operative children will not feel obliged to follow orders from those with whom they are not close or who are not perceived as representing authority. The feeling of respect, which guides obligation, is developed by two concomitant feelings: love and fear.

> A mixed feeling, thirdly, composed of both affection and fear: this is the feeling of respect, whose exceptional importance in the formation or

> exercise of moral conscience has been emphasized by all moralists. For some, respect is a derived affective state that is unique in its kind: it doesn't have other individuals as its object, like love or fear, but is directly linked to the values or moral laws embodied in those individuals; respecting a person would consist of respecting the moral law in that individual (Kant), or the discipline he represents and applies (Durkheim). According to other authors with whom we are affiliated, respect, while remaining susceptible to taking on secondary, higher forms, is first and foremost, like the other two, a feeling from individual to individual and is like the mixture of affection and fear that children experience in relation to their parents (PIAGET, 1977, p. 72-73).

So neither love nor fear alone can develop a sense of respect. The heteronomous child, who is spared the rules and orders of adults, may have no notion of limits. Imposing rules, in the Piagetian approach, is not coercion, but enforcing conventions that are useful for mutual well-being. As Piaget (1932/1994) says, "moral coercion is a very close relative of intellectual coercion" (p. 93). In addition, we must consider that affection is a preponderant element in building a sense of respect. For children to feel safe, accepted and loved, they need to comply with the adult's commands.

At the stage of moral heteronomy, norms are governed by the other, the one who represents authority. The nomia, the norm, is still external to the subject or "hetero", because it is in the other. At this point, respect is unilateral and not mutual. Compliance with norms is still marked by obedience to authority, which is not necessarily a bad thing. However, obedience without reflection on one's actions, combined with other authoritarian experiences, can contribute to the heteronomy stage lasting into adulthood. Piaget did not claim that moral heteronomy was only characteristic of children, although he did point out that it indicates a stage of morality in which reciprocity is not present or appears to be at a disadvantage.

The heteronomous subject reveals their inability to have moral feelings because they don't realize the obligation, not the obligation to obey the other, but in the sense of self-management, which in turn considers the common good and the need for mutual respect. In the heteronomy stage, moral conduct adopts the perspective of the other, of what has been imposed or taught. The figure of authority is, in this period, necessary for the fulfillment of norms and for their control and maintenance. Even though they are out of sight of those who represent authority, when they act in accordance with moral norms, they do so for the sake of the other, for the sake of those who may represent the law, who may punish them or threaten to punish them, and not for their own reasons. Heteronomy in adulthood is also revealed through actions that are only practiced in the sight of the other, such as respecting traffic laws, if at the mercy of the traffic warden, or not dirtying a public place because you are in the company of someone who controls such action.

Pre-morality is also marked by moral realism. Children in the pre-operational cognitive stage, marked by heteronomy and no longer by anomie (because they already know the rules and attribute an authoritative value to them), understand that the rules are obligatory and attribute a value to the facts that overrides the intention of the person who caused the problem or damage. At this point, the child has an egocentric mindset, which leads them to interpret the rules as something good, since they are defined by the adult, who must be obeyed, because this is what is correct and expected. Thus, in a given situation, the damage caused is interpreted on the basis of the realism of the situation, only the observable reality is evaluated literally. The concept of responsibility is objective, because the judgment is based on the consequences of the acts and not on their intentionality, according to research by Piaget (1932/1994).

The author analyzed how children judge the problems they face in their daily lives, presenting them with the following question: who is more to blame, someone who unknowingly knocks over and breaks ten cups that were behind the door, by running in, or someone who breaks a single cup, trying to pick up the tin of sweets that their mother had forbidden them to eat? The child, while still in the moral realism stage, blames the person who knocked over the ten cups, disregarding the intention and attributing more value to the material damage, in other words, they are driven by the magnitude of the damage, since breaking ten cups is seen as more serious than breaking just one. It's worth pointing out that the answers given by children to hypothetical situations, with no direct connection to them, can lead them not only to different conclusions but also to different actions, if and when this situation occurs in their lives or involves them. Moral thinking and moral action can therefore diverge, since in the same study, Piaget found that some children, whose answers blamed the person who caused the most material damage, also considered lying and deceiving others to be serious.

Thus, in the answers given to the stories, moral realism is evident, disqualifying intention, even when the children are already able to tell stories in which guilt follows lying or cheating, demonstrating a clear distinction between the two levels of moral thinking: action and ideas. Even so, reflecting on moral dilemmas or problems gives children the opportunity to think about how to respond, what is right or wrong, even hypothetically. It is even more important to provide such opportunities if the problem being discussed has been experienced by the child, as it is important for them to be the author of the solution to their problems, always in a non-coercive way. In fact, if reflection accompanies conflict resolution and takes into account the other person's point of view, new possibilities for development will be opened up towards autonomous morality. It should be clear, however, that developing cognitively does not mean developing morally. Developing morally, on the other hand, requires mental structures that allow for complex challenges in the field of cognition. Recognizing different points of view involves, for example, the mental exercise of operant relationships, such as feelings of reciprocity, empathy or even dialogue.

Children in the cognitive stage of concrete operations - from approximately seven to eleven years of age - are able to reverse their thinking, achieving logical deducibility, which Piaget calls the reversibility of thought. Before this stage, ten toothpicks lined up and ten of them overlapping, in two sets side by side, mean different quantities to a child in the pre-operational stage. In the same way, two hundred milliliters of water poured into a wider, lower container also means less liquid than two hundred milliliters in a tall, narrow bottle. The reversibility of thought lies precisely in distinguishing different relationships between classes. In this sense, in a class of flowers, if we separate six daisies, four roses and two chrysanthemums, when we ask a child, who is unable to reverse his thinking, which of them appears in greater quantity, he will be able to answer that it is the daisies. However, if we ask them whether there are more daisies or flowers, their answer will be daisies, because including daisies in the flowers class is a very difficult task for a pre-operative child. In the next stage, these facts will no longer be observed.

A child in the operative stage is able to make estimates, such as measuring a space that holds a certain number of objects or people and calculating approximately how many will fit in this space. It would be possible for an 8 or 9 year old child, for example, to say how many pieces of a new nesting game - similar in size to a Lego[2] - are in a jar that previously held her two hundred pieces of Lego. It is expected that the child will relate their previous experience, which considers space and quantity, to the estimate made, answering that there should be approximately 200 Lego sticks. Reversing this thought, i.e. using previous knowledge for a new problem and realizing that what has been done can be undone, are operative skills.

Calculating how many people are present at a demonstration follows the same principle. Data such as the demonstration on December 16, 2015, in favor of the *impeachment of* President Dilma Rousseff, indicated the presence of three thousand participants, later corrected to fifty thousand, according to the newspaper O Estado de Sao Paulo, on December 17, 2015. Even though schools do little work on estimation, avoiding dealing with abstractions and

[2] Lego refers to a toy made up of a series of pegs that can be fitted together to form various objects, depending on who wants to put them together.

therefore making it difficult to understand the results and also the possibilities of being wrong, a child who is an operator, if given the opportunity to learn about this notion and experience a cognitive conflict with it, may well be able to carry out such calculations in smaller spaces, for example, than Avenida Paulista.

Reversibility in thinking makes it possible to consider different points of view, since the same situation can have different meanings depending on who is analyzing it. The example that asks about the amount of liquid in different bottles and the one that asks whether there are more flowers or daisies can already be understood by children at the stage of concrete operations:

> These problems and others are more easily solved by the fact that increasing internalizations, coordinations and decentralizations lead to a general form of equilibrium that constitutes operant reversibility (inversions and reciprocities). (PIAGET, 1975, p. 40).

Even though reversibility in thought is already a condition of the subject's cognitive structure, it affects objects or their presence in a concrete way, because the conditions for acting on the basis of hypotheses are still rudimentary. As egocentrism is no longer present, the subject is able to put themselves in the other person's shoes and consider different ideas and hypotheses.

The mental action of the operational child requires concrete experimentation and acting on situations and objects. This is as true of a history lesson as it is of a science lesson: the teacher's observation of a scientific experiment is of little use, as is the discussion of hypotheses about moral issues. Of course, everything can be discussed and the discourse itself can indicate an understanding of what is considered correct or inappropriate. However, the construction of concepts requires concrete experience, of what the child lives or has lived through, such as participating in school assemblies, where the students themselves bring up issues for discussion. (ARAUJO; PUIG; ARANTES, 2007)

The stage of formal operations, starting around the age of eleven or twelve, at the beginning of adolescence, reveals an intellectual maturation that no longer focuses on objects, but on hypotheses. Their intellectual capacity allows them to make inferences that take into account not only representable realities, but also other people's ideas, i.e. also hypotheses. There is a new way of reasoning, in which mental operations go beyond considering the premise as part of the particular, an ability acquired in the operative stage. In the premises A=B and B=C, therefore A=C or every prisoner has acted against morality and broken the law, therefore every prisoner is immoral, deductive thinking has already been built and can evolve into inductive thinking. In this case, in addition to the deductions, it is possible to consider particular issues for each case, because not every premise fits every case.

Thus, a prisoner can serve time because he considers universal ethical principles above the conventions of the law, which does not make him immoral. Disrespecting the law in the name of universal ethical principles, such as the preservation of human life, is not considered immoral, so in inductive thinking, such details are considered and not just generalizations. The search for reasons to justify a judgment is already a cognitive skill. As in the previous example, at the stage of formal operations, it is already possible to ask why that person was arrested, under what circumstances they committed the crime, etc. Formulating these questions makes it possible to think about the variables that make up a statement and to draw conclusions from them. This is different from the previous cognitive stage - that of concrete operations - when the premise is enough to justify the statement: if he's in prison, then he's immoral.

Although the intellectual condition in the formal operant stage offers a cognitive structure for inductive thinking, the role of the social environment and cognitive conflicts, which will occur throughout the subject's life, will have a significant impact on the development of an intelligence that goes beyond the limits of the obvious. Neither formal operational thinking nor external contributions are guarantees of intellectual development in terms of morality. According to Piaget (1975), the school plays a fundamental role in the balances that will provide subsidies for new mental operations. The author states that:

> This operativity is neither pre-formed once and for all nor can it be explained by external contributions from experience or social transmission: it is the product of successive constructions, and the main factor in this constructivism is a balance through self-regulation that allows momentary inconsistencies to be remedied, problems to be solved and crises to be overcome (PIAGET, 1975, p. 49).

In this sense, a school environment that encourages choice and problem-solving will promote autonomy by allowing the subject to think for themselves and make their ideas complex, adopting a perspective that transcends personal desire to reach the collective view, an essential aspect of moral autonomy.

3.4 Affectivity

For Piaget (1932/1994), affectivity plays a preponderant role in the formation of intelligence. If the factors of cognitive development are a cognitive structure capable of enhancing biological maturation, physical and social experience, affectivity is the spring that drives the desire to know, a necessary condition for learning. Desire can be seen through different prisms, but here we will stick to the Piagetian view that desire is what drives the subject's actions towards the object. Based on the premise that knowledge occurs through the subject's action on the object[3] , transforming it, displacing it, combining it and bringing it together again, this action must be desired by the subject. The mechanism of action can take place by impulse, for example, if the subject is in the sensorimotor stage, it is not uncommon to observe that they are walking, apparently at random. However, this is a false notion, because children walk because they want to explore the world around them, even if they don't realize it. A person in the formal operative stage, who is interested, for example, in entering a renowned university, even if he is not curious about the content covered in the entrance exam, may, in the name of a greater desire - to enter university - be able to make use of it, concentrating on what will allow him to achieve his goal: study.

Discussions on morality offer vast ground for analyzing the affective subject, since dissociating the rational from the affective in a discussion on values would be an impossible task. According to La Taille, Kohl and Dantas (1992):

> A good way of understanding and evaluating a particular author's articulation between affectivity and intelligence is to analyze his conceptions on the subject of moral judgment. In fact, human morality is the stage par excellence on which affectivity and reason generally meet in the form of a confrontation (p. 47).

Literature, art and philosophy offer many examples for reflection on the relationship between the affective and the rational. A good example is the play "The Tempest" by the English playwright William Shakespeare, first staged in 1611. In it, the character Prospero - Duke of Milan, is forcibly taken, along with his daughter Miranda, to a desert island, as a strategy to depose him from his political post, through an alliance between his brother Antonio and Alonso, King of Naples. On this island, Prospero becomes powerful when he takes possession of a witch's books, studies them and becomes a magician. Possessing great powers, he creates a storm so that his brother Antonio, Alonso and the entire crew are shipwrecked, while ensuring that no one dies in it. Prospero foresees his daughter Miranda's love match with Alonso's son, their falling in love and many other plots that fill this 17th century story. The play involves discussions of various concepts that can be interpreted in different ways, including revenge, justice, love and forgiveness. Now, if the betrayal suffered by Prospero and,

---

[3] The object is understood in Piagetian terms as something material and tangible, as well as knowledge, ideas and social experiences.

dialectically, his desire to see his daughter live a great love with the son of the man who had removed him from power, lead the duke to cause the storm. Couldn't we also find similar situations in real stories, which change the choices made in the moral field? The rationality that, when faced with a problem situation, makes it possible to raise hypotheses, reflect, construct alternative courses of action, plan, implement and evaluate them also implies knowing the feelings that move people. In this way, rationality is directly linked to and driven by affective relationships. Literature, the stage for the plots of human beings, albeit in the form of fiction, intertwines philosophical reflections with affective and rational aspects which are, in the Piagetian view, interconnected, because they act together: affectivity is the energy that moves the action of thought.

3.5 The concept of morality

The definition of morality has been the subject of long debates and reflections since ancient times. Philosophers have grappled with ideas about what represents morality, a discussion that is far from over. Socrates warned that a thoughtless life was not worth living. In this way, any action by human beings in their social environment that does not take relationships into account, that is based only on themselves and not on the other, or on the common good, is hardly worthwhile. Piaget's (1932/1994) studies on morality were dedicated to assessing how children think about moral rules, how they judge them and what they say about them. Piaget defines morality as follows:

> All morality consists of a system of rules and the essence of all morality must be sought in the respect that the individual acquires for these rules (PIAGET, 1932/1994, p. 23).

From this perspective, morality is the law, it is what guides people's actions, based on their social and temporal reality. Piaget didn't expand his studies to include moral action, instead focusing on understanding the ways in which individuals understand what is right or wrong, or what is good or bad.

If mathematics, literature or science are socially constructed, so are morals. Morality cannot be intuited, in other words, reflection on a given action or the choice of what is considered morally correct (or reprehensible) cannot be acquired through immediate apprehension; it is always a social construction, regardless of the age of the individual. Exact, human or biological sciences are taught at school in order to form people. Morals, on the other hand, are learned in the family, at school and in wider social life. But the school institution in particular, because it allows for different interactions between teachers and students, is a favorable and efficient setting for the development of moral thinking.

3.6 Moral education

Moral and civic education[4] (EMC), taught in schools during Brazil's military dictatorship, was marked by a set of values and political interests that sought to promote social control and repression. The EMC curriculum authoritatively laid down moral guidelines, i.e. what should and shouldn't be done, and saw disagreement or debate as a lack of civility and a lack of education on the part of those who valued it. No wonder obedience and servile behavior were indicative of a good student. Moral and civic lessons, in addition to emphasizing national symbols, aimed to convince the population that obeying was an honorable attitude and worthy of good men. Some content praised the role of the military as a collaborator of justice and the common good, an idea that advocated society adopting the same format as the army, marked by the strong hierarchization of roles and powers. From this perspective, the vision of the cordial man seemed to contribute to the political moment of the time, precisely because it maintained the dictatorship. In this way, school education would also benefit this form of government if it trained men who did not question the status quo.

In the context of the dictatorship, classroom methodology meant that they had to be expository, because, after all, the "holder of knowledge" was the master, as the teacher was called at the time, who valued the quiet student, who passively copied the links on the blackboard and who only answered when asked by the teacher. Even so, the answers had to follow the standard in force. It is worth noting that the lecture in itself is not synonymous with the traditional teaching method, since the teacher, in the constructivist view, also represents authority and leadership. In this way, it is not the lecture that encourages the student not to be questioning, but what happens after the lecture, i.e. whether or not the student can present and discuss their ideas. In the EMC, and other school moments during the dictatorship, reworking, innovating and creating were not guarantees of good school results, while following the standard proposed by the teacher was.

From this perspective, which saw the student playing a passive role, it wasn't a problem

[4] On September 12, 1969, Decree-Law No. 869 was repealed. Article 1 of this law provides for the inclusion of Moral and Civic Education as a compulsory subject and Article 2 defines that the workload allocated to the subjects of Moral and Civic Education, Social and Political Organization of Brazil and Studies of Brazilian Problems, in the curricula of primary, secondary and higher education, is intended to form citizenship and knowledge of the Brazilian reality.

if their moral autonomy wasn't promoted, keeping them in the heteronomous stage. The relationships experienced in the physical environment, with the conflicts they engender, are the privileged components of intelligence, which is essential for the development of moral autonomy, the ability to think, to put oneself in another's shoes, to understand and respect the different ways of understanding the world, to support and learn from diversity.

Contrary to the principles that justified the inclusion of EMC in the school curriculum during the leaden years of the military dictatorship, when it came to an end, another perspective on moral education was adopted. Although schools present the most renowned thinkers and a set of contents to be covered in order to promote moral development, the formation of a person with ethical principles and moral attitudes cannot be guaranteed. The study of philosophy and debates about world reality can be strong allies for critical thinking. However, in constructivist education, it is understood that it is through everyday conflicts and the way in which they are resolved that the ethical formation of children and young people actually contributes.

> Is it intended to train individuals who are subject to the oppression of traditions and previous generations? In that case, the authority of the teacher and, possibly, the 'links' of morality, with the system of encouragement and punitive sanctions, are enough to reinforce this morality of obedience. On the contrary, do we want to train both free consciences and individuals who respect the rights and freedom of others? Only social life among the pupils themselves, i.e. self-government taken as far as possible and parallel to intellectual work in common, can lead to this dual development of personalities who are masters of themselves and of their mutual respect. (PIAGET, 1977, p. 71).

In the book "Where education is going" (PIAGET, 1977), Piaget recounts an experience he had during a visit between 1930 and 1935 to an institution for juvenile delinquents in Eastern Europe. The director, contrary to any educational system of the time, entrusted the children and adolescents with the discipline of the institution. These students set up a court inside the institution, which was fully staffed by the inmates. Anyone caught acting against the house's regulations was judged by the juvenile penal chamber and the conduct of the judges was to welcome, regenerate and reintegrate them, entrusting them with a job. The inmates' regeneration was not immediate, which is natural, but through the trust that was established, combined with strategies that provided for reciprocal sanctions, good results were obtained in the attitudes of these young inmates. One of these strategies was the production of a newspaper in which the deliberations and sentences were published. This newspaper was possibly destroyed during one of the battles in Varsovia. Piaget reports that:

> There is nothing more exciting for the psychologist than this document: the humanity, the understanding, the subtlety of the evaluation of these adolescent judges, themselves delinquents, had something moving and comforting about it. (PIAGET, 1977, p. 78)

Goergen (2007) corroborates the precepts of moral autonomy. He talks about moral education and the importance of the school in this regard, without diminishing the responsibility of all social bodies, such as the family, the media, etc. However, this is not a simple task, but rather a rethinking of the concepts of citizenship, democracy, social justice and public space.

Human beings are endowed with rationality, and in this condition they are capable of fighting to win their freedom, not a freedom permeated by actions that disregard others, but a freedom that reveals a state of sovereignty and independence, revealed by their autonomy: "[...] there is no freedom without justice, nor justice without freedom" (GOERGEN, 2007, p. 754). The moral subject is the one who considers their individual freedom, but not least the values and norms of society, so that it is dignified and just: "Justice is the first and most fundamental virtue of contemporary man." (GOERGEN, 2007, p. 754).

3.7 Socio-moral environment

School is a place where children learn to relate to each other, to live with others, forming lakes, enmities and sympathies, a space where, based on the gaze of others, they also begin the process of identity, organizing ideas about who they are, what role they occupy in that social group and also what the rules are that organize it. By choice or neglect, the school establishes a socio-moral environment, according to Devries and Zan (1998):

> The socio-moral environment is the entire network of interpersonal relationships that make up a child's school experience. This experience includes the child's relationship with the teacher, with other children, with their studies and with the rules (p. 17).

In the light of this idea, every school has a socio-moral environment based on reciprocity and mutual respect or, on the contrary, on authoritarianism and obedience. The constructivist socio-moral environment aims to establish a living space based on mutual respect. It's not about moral education in the sense of indoctrination, but rather about establishing interpersonal relationships marked by fairness and a good relationship with knowledge and dialogical practices. Some actions planned by the school - here understood as the whole community: parents, students, teachers, other professionals and local society - strengthen this possibility, cooperation, the opportunity to choose based on the common good and mutual respect offer students the challenge of acting responsibly and knowing how to deal with the consequences of their decisions. Choosing is a difficult task because it involves judgment. In order to choose, you need to be clear that every choice always involves losses, and you need to identify what you don't want to lose. However, in interpersonal relationships you also have to consider the other person's losses.

In a teaching system that promotes cooperation, collective decisions are the core of the work and conflicts are inevitable. From a Piagetian perspective, however, conflicts are opportunities for development and learning. It should be emphasized that by valuing the role of conflict, the constructivist environment does not promote a climate of constant warfare. On the contrary, as in the institution visited by Piaget between 1930 and 1935, cooperation created an atmosphere conducive to the teaching-learning process, which involved everyone, creating a space based on dialog and respect.

In this socio-moral environment, the teacher is responsible for developing strategies to help students self-regulate, making sure that breaks in cooperation are re-established whenever necessary. According to Devries and Zan (1998), one of these strategies is for the rules to be established by the students themselves:

> The social and moral rules constructed by children themselves are rooted in their day-to-day personal experiences. These personal experiences with peers and adults lead them to build cause and effect relationships between their actions and also to predict the reactions of others (p. 193).

3.8 Rules and their importance

Piaget (1932/1994) analyzed how children of different ages understood rules and the feeling of obligation they established. To do this, he observed children playing games, one of which was marbles. In a game situation, players have the opportunity to relate to a complex system of rules, to adapt (or not) to this system, to accept it and follow it, or even to try to change it, with or without the other person's consent. In short, when you play with rules, you are living a moral system. The rules of play and the rules of coexistence are different, because the rules of play can be established by the children and the rules of coexistence are imposed by the social group. In general, adults allow or correct children's attitudes that are not in line with what is expected by the social group. Although the rules of games and the norms of coexistence are different in nature, they are still rules or obligations that are external to the child. At the stage of moral heteronomy, complying with the rule determined by the older child or adult is seen as the right thing to do. At this stage, the principle that justifies the rule is not common knowledge, although it is possible to understand that if there is a rule, it is expected that it will be complied with.

When rules are constructed by children, especially in the school environment, they enable self-regulation and therefore reduce heteronomy. By taking on the role of the one who sets the rules (and thus being forced to deal with the wishes of others), moral autonomy is exercised. Devries and Zan (1998) point out that, in general, the adult - or the teacher - is afraid to delegate this prerogative to the child, believing that they could construct inappropriate rules. However, the authors argue that:

> These fears have not been borne out in our experiences of observing young children as they participate in setting rules. Of course, the constructivist teacher doesn't hand everything over to the children: instead, he or she exercises leadership by guiding the rule-setting process and the development of children's attitudes and knowledge about rule-setting (p. 138).

The rules of the games researched by Piaget, observing or playing marbles with children, resulted in the establishment of four stages. The first stage is the sensorimotor period, which is purely based on motor skills and sensations. In this stage, the child manipulates the balls according to their desires and motor possibilities, so it can't be said that collective rules are used at this point. In the second stage, which takes place around the pre-operational period, also called egocentric, the child is able to imitate the rules, i.e. they receive them from others and exercise them, but without worrying about winning or losing, the "I" occupies a central role, so that they don't consider who reached the objective of the game first. In the third stage, around the age of seven or eight (concrete operations), there is already a desire to beat opponents by controlling the rules. However, this mastery can vary, because in Piaget's research (1932/1994) it was common to find different and sometimes contradictory explanations of the rules of the same game, indicating that if there is interest and concern for the rules, the conventions may not yet be understood as collective agreements, subject to change only in the face of a new consensus. In the fourth stage, called codification of the rules, around the age of eleven or twelve, at the beginning of the formal operative period, the rules are known by everyone. The desire to cooperate also appears at this stage, when discussions are not only about understanding the rule and/or maintaining it, but also about mutual agreements:

> Children in the fourth stage, on the other hand, know their code in depth and even enjoy legal discussions, whether in-depth or concerning simple procedures, which

can arise when they have doubts (PIAGET, 1932/1994, p. 44).

Discussions about the rules and their use are necessary and intrinsic aspects of the game, a situation that favors a complex social experience that is not so different from the social life of adults.

3.9 Moral autonomy

Playing games helps them to understand the rules and the role of collective agreements and, to this extent, can be an ally in experimenting with the social world, offering cognitive and interpersonal resources for decentering, stepping out of one's own perspective to consider that of the other. Decentering oneself is an activity that can only be carried out by someone who has already reached the period of concrete operations, who has appropriated and surpassed the possibilities of the pre-operational stage. In fact, putting oneself in the other person's shoes is practically impossible for the egocentric child, even if they are capable of repeating what they already know is the right thing to do. But this knowledge is only restricted to discourse. When you have the cognitive conditions to decentralize and thus understand the other person's point of view, why can't you go beyond your own perspective? Moral autonomy is not achieved simultaneously with cognitive development. According to Vinha (2000) moral autonomy is:

> The ability to govern oneself; it is necessary that it is inserted in an environment of mutual respect, in which the authoritarianism of the adult is minimized and the individuals who relate to each other consider themselves as equals and respect each other. (p. 18-19).

If intellectual development does not guarantee moral development, heteronomous subjects exist in moral terms regardless of their age. If the school wants to develop morally autonomous subjects, it needs to reflect on the system of sanctions adopted by adults or institutions. Representing authority is part of the teacher's role, something that is not harmful if it is not based on authoritarianism. In fact, sanctions are part of any educational system, as they imply the possibility of educating individuals and leading them to decentralize. However, there are sanctions and sanctions: some are detrimental to moral development and others contribute to the democratic maintenance of collective agreements, as they favor mutual respect. Piaget (1932/1994) states that "moral coercion is a very close relative of intellectual coercion" (p. 93) and establishes two types of sanctions: expiatory and reciprocal.

The word sanction indicates a penalty to be carried out by someone who performs an act disapproved of by the criminal or political system, as well as a breach of agreements. Sanctions are related to justice because they are seen as inappropriate when they punish an innocent person or fail to punish a guilty person. Thus, justice or injustice is also evaluated based on the sanctions that are established. In this way, they can be positive in a social system that provides for consequences for those who don't follow the rules. These consequences can come from a democratic system (in which people jointly set the rules) or from an authoritarian system (in which the sanction is prescribed by someone).

When a mistake is made, it's common for sanctions to be imposed by authority figures or by the group itself. There are those who err and admit their mistakes, but there are also those who deny, apologize, omit or even accuse other people. A good example of a mistake is one linked to everyday situations, such as not showing up for a previously agreed-upon appointment. When you notice someone else's mistake, different reactions are triggered in the person who made the mistake. If the injured party accuses the other of wrongdoing, it's possible that a feeling of anger will be created in the wrongdoer, as if this were an exaggerated or unnecessary reaction. Possibly, the offenses and accusations would be returned, in an attempt to take the focus off the mistake and onto the accuser. Decentralization does not occur in these circumstances, because there is no attempt to put oneself in the other person's shoes. Fights and searches for who is most to blame ensue, and we stop learning from the mistake. But when the other person is told that the wait caused embarrassment and concern, that they were afraid something serious had happened, and when the "offender" explains themselves, acknowledges their mistake and perhaps apologizes, there is a mutual exercise in decentralization, through which both parties are able to consider the other's perspective.

Sanction, when it makes use of fear, threat, exposure, accusation or punishment, is of the expiatory type. For Bagat (1986 apud VINHA, 2000):

> Expiatory sanctions are characterized by coercion and an arbitrary nature, with no relationship between the content of the sanction and the act being sanctioned. As the name implies, its aim is to make the person who has broken a rule, or committed an undesirable act, suffer, to atone for their mistake; seeking to provoke maximum psychobiophysical discomfort (p. 350).

Piaget warns that an education that aims to develop moral autonomy should not resort to expiatory sanction to enforce the adult's authority. In fact, the sanction that comes from the other person can generate feelings of conformity or revolt, and there is little point in making amends for the mistake. Escaping punishment is a very recurrent possibility in a system in which expiatory sanction is established. A teacher who asks a group of students who has committed a fault, such as clogging the toilets with rolls of toilet paper, and threatens them with missing recess if the culprit doesn't come forward, provokes - depending on their age - collective punishment, the delinquency of the classmate or the breakdown of the relationships of trust that exist between them. The expiatory sanction seeks the culprit and atonement for the error, rather than reparation, a situation that favors moral heteronomy. The rules and their maintenance are not in the subject, but outside him, in the other, in the one who can punish. Not infrequently, this system increases the possibility that students will try not to be found out, encouraging dishonesty and the avoidance of their faults. Speeches such as: "If I catch the person who did this...", or "If you want to make a mistake, do it right, because if you get caught...", implicitly teach students not to put themselves in the other person's shoes, but to avoid making up for their own mistakes. Reciprocal sanctions, on the other hand, according to Piaget (1932/1994):

> They go hand in hand with cooperation and the rules of equality. Whether it's a rule that the child accepts from within, i.e. has understood that it binds them to their peers by a link of reciprocity (for example, don't lie, because lying makes mutual trust impossible, etc.), if the rule is violated, there is absolutely no need to repress it.) If the rule is violated, there is absolutely no need, in order to put things back in order, for painful repression to impose respect for the law from outside: it is enough that the rupture of the social link, caused by the guilty party, makes its effects felt; in other words, it is enough to make reciprocity work (p. 161-162).

When the lack of fulfillment of the commitment is discussed, exposing concern and feelings of embarrassment, the heart of the problem lies in the failure to keep the agreement. Through the perception of the other person and the consequences caused, a solution to the problem is sought. Reciprocity implies considering one's own perspectives as well as those of the other person, so that sanctions of this nature motivate the repair of the error. At school, when the teacher comes across pupils who have blocked the toilet and tells them about the damage to property, the carelessness of the cleaners, the accumulation of tasks, etc., without asking who did it and, at the same time, requesting the help of volunteers to repair the situation, it is possible to imagine a different attitude on the part of the pupils. Facing up to the factual consequences of the problem is important for the feeling of reciprocity: hearing from the person responsible how it feels to clean a clogged toilet, or from the person who deals with the financial sector about the costs of hygiene materials, can help students to get their heads around the fact that actions cause damage and that it's important to consider them next time.

Certainly, the practice of reciprocal sanctions requires a lot more time from the school to solve a problem. Expiatory sanctions require little. It is worth considering, however, that if adults act like children in their family or professional environment, trying to escape the consequences of their actions, perhaps it is up to the school to devote more time to resolving conflicts, getting people to put themselves in the other person's shoes.

Araujo, Puig and Arantes (2007) emphasize the importance of dialogue in the school environment. They argue that resolving conflicts in a dialogic and cooperative way is also a task for the school, with a view to forming autonomous human beings capable of dealing ethically with personal and social conflicts. One of the ways the authors present as an alternative for the school to deal with this moral learning, based on psychological knowledge of oneself and others, is school assemblies. This is a democratic space for resolving conflicts, taking into account moral and ethical values, enabling the school to bring moments of reflection and dialog into its daily life, in these meetings planned and led by the school, but giving the students a voice.

3.10 The concept of ethics

Jean Piaget's contribution to moral education is undeniably a reference for countless reflections in the field of ethics. Although the concepts studied by Piaget in this field are about the development and moral judgment of children, they serve as a foundation for reflection on ethical principles and their role in society for both children and adults. For Piaget (1977), interpersonal relationships are the foundations of moral development, as he believes that it is in relationships with others that heteronomous and later autonomous attitudes are built. Ethics can be interpreted as a set of moral choices for the common good (note here the importance given to the social dimension, because in isolation there can be no ëP^), so that social relationships are necessary for moral exercise. On a higher level, choosing to practice ethics implies seeking to establish an environment of mutual respect and cooperation.

Piaget (1977) indicates that morality, at a certain point in moral development, begins by being external to the subject, seen as unilateral respect, whose internalization evolves into mutual respect: "At the other extreme of inter-individual relationships, which form moral values, is mutual respect." (p. 75). For the author, respect is the origin of morality and can also be seen as a ethical principle. Talking about ethics, from a Piagetian perspective, means thinking about self-government. When discussing the type of education that offers the development of moral autonomy, the author considers that the best way to achieve this goal is to give school and, more precisely, social life, more opportunities to make choices about social conventions, rather than simply obeying them. In this sense, the concepts of cooperation are the foundations for a "good life" (ethics) in a group:

> The first of these processes is moral coercion by the adult, which results in heteronomy and, consequently, moral realism. The second is cooperation, which results in autonomy (PIAGET, 1932/1994, p. 154).

La Taille (1993), for his part, combines the idea of cooperation with duty:

> Now, the duty to be cooperative cannot be conceived as a hypothetical duty because the idea of cooperation is underpinned by the idea of equality, which is a moral - and political - value. The duty to be cooperative is therefore an absolute duty: cooperation, a value in itself, can be followed regardless of its technical effectiveness. (p. 81)

If moral duty occupies a place in the practice of ethics, because to be ëb^ ë one must fulfill moral duties, the word cooperation, as its root[5] suggests, can be interpreted as a joint operation that transcends morality. Here's an example: it is a moral duty and also a law in the Brazilian Constitution (1988) to respect and not discriminate against people for their religious choices, according to Articles 1 and 20. However, it is not a moral duty to cooperate with the victim who has experienced this situation. Based on Piaget's reflections, it is possible to attribute a ëb^ level to the action of cooperating free of charge with someone discriminated against because of their religion and collaborating with them, using freedom of choice on an ethical level, which is that of living well with oneself and socially. It is worth pointing out that if such cooperation seeks praise, prestige, exemption from coercion or any other reward, it is not autonomous action, but heteronomous. In cooperation based on moral autonomy, the relationship is one of equality and reciprocity. In this case, cooperation is not based on a feeling of superiority for helping someone and/or obedience to conventions or leaders.

Kohlberg, in his book *"Kohlberg's Approach to Moral Education"* and Power, Higgins and Kohlberg (1989, apud DEVRIES; ZAN, 1998) describe a "just community", established through the use of ethical standards that would be tested in schools and in a women's penitentiary. Kohlberg was not content with studying the stages of moral judgment and discussing their dilemmas; he was also concerned with understanding whether (and how) more evolved moral judgments affect people's actual behavior. The "just community" provided for democratic decision-making, i.e. without a hierarchical gap - teacher/student - that valued local culture and encouraged conflict resolution, in an approach that "fits in with the Durkheimian conception of collectivism" (DURKHEIM, [18--?] apud BIAGGIO, 2006, p. 48). In the

[5] Cooperation is formed by the prefix 'co', which means 'together'. Operation, on the other hand, means action, actuation, a word that comes from the Latin *'operatione'*, which, with the prefix 'co' indicates action together.

practice of the "Just Community", the evolutionary stages of moral judgment were taken into account, so that they were carefully destabilized through cognitive conflicts, which promoted their evolution to the next stages. Everyday situations were used, on the assumption made by Kohlberg that they would be more conducive to the transposition of judgment into real behavior. This shows the understanding given by Piaget and Kohlberg to the principles of equality, cooperation and mutual respect.

Whether in philosophy or common sense, diction has been - and still is - tirelessly discussed, with different meanings being attributed to it. This is how philosopher Clovis de Barros Filho and Julio Pompeu (2013) see it:

> Ethics is about living together. That is its object. But its understanding and comprehension also imply intellectual effort, because it is thinking about shared life, about social relations. It's a knowledge that mobilizes, that comes from the other and which, curiously, is absent from our formal education. (p. 19).

Following Filho and Pompeu's (2013) assertion about ethics and coexistence, the social ambit is present in the different conceptualizations. However, this social aspect of coexistence, inherent to ethics, does not imply that it is learned simply because everyone lives in society. Discourses on ethics are often seen as demagogic. The cross-cutting themes of the National Curriculum Parameters (PCN) (BRASIL, 1997), show ethics as a cross-cutting theme to be discussed in the classroom, which doesn't seem to have materialized in the vast majority of primary and secondary schools in Brazil. In this sense, it seems more than necessary and absolutely essential for society to reflect on coexistence and ethics in a broad sense, also including in this reflection the role of choices, of active participation in school decisions, in ways of thinking that can go beyond personal interests.

Ethics (understood as good living, i.e. choices that bring emotional comfort) should not be confused with happiness. In fact, ethical choices tend to be difficult and sometimes cause great suffering. Choosing always implies abandoning other possibilities and, therefore, losses. Ethical and moral education must therefore be part of human formation. According to Casassus (2009), this education involves many difficulties, as it takes place through cultural aspects that interfere with observing and judging others:

> In some cultures, such as Japan, it is not polite to express emotions and people are taught to smile on any occasion. They even define what they should and shouldn't feel; this leads to the denial of emotions even in front of oneself (p. 197).

It is possible to draw an analogy between ethics and the (affective) meaning it gains for the individual in their educational process. In fact, what provokes feelings of fear or shame can already be considered an ethical imperative. If something has to be done in secret, out of shame or fear of the other person's judgment, this is a premise of ethics, because it violates moral duty. However, La Taille (2006) warns that the relationship between reason and affectivity deserves to be analyzed more carefully. The influence of emotion on reason or decision-making cannot be radically attributed. Although it's more common to find more generous attitudes when people are happy and, conversely, less forgiving attitudes in situations of suffering, generalizations are unwarranted.

> In short, it seems to me that there is no point in talking about a supposed 'emotional intelligence' - unless you want to limit yourself to giving a pompous name to the contextual variability of various skills, including moral ones, instead of actually shedding some light on the perennial links between judgment and the will to act according to its dictates (LA TAILLE, 2006, p. 66).

La Taille (2006) indicates that the concept of ethics is part of the answer to the question "what life do I want to live?" referring to the good life or happiness. The ethical plane indicates self-expansion, which stems from the motivation or desire to act in accordance with the moral plane, based on the feeling of obligation. From then on, the feeling of shame and annoyance at betraying what is considered moral is no longer dependent on the gaze or judgment of others, making up the ethical plane. Self-expansion also implies going beyond self-esteem understood as self-worth, since this includes self-respect, an essential aspect for practicing mutual respect.

Cortella (2010) defines ethics as "what marks the frontier of our coexistence." (p. 105). To define ethics, the same author asks three questions: do I want to, should I and can I have a happy life? The set of values that guides these answers involves ethics and, if they are positive, it is possible to think of an ethical life, in other words, a happy life.

> There are things I want, but I shouldn't. There are things I should, but don't want to. When do you have peace of mind? When you have a little happiness? When what you want is what you should and what you can (CORTELLA, 2010, p. 107).

> And where does the word ethics come from? From the Greek *ethos* which, until the 6th century BC, meant "human dwelling". The Latin expression *'domus'* is a translation of the Greek *ethos*. *Ethos* is the place where we live, it's our home (CORTELLA, 2010, p. 106).

3.11 Ethical personality

In order to approach the ethical personality, it is important to highlight two concepts: the moral plane and the ethical plane. La Taille (2006) postulates that the concept of morality[6] refers to a set of rules, so that when faced with the question "how should I act?", the psychological motivation is, on a moral level, the feeling of obligation. However, intellectual and affective conditions are necessary, without dissociating them, since affectivity represents a pulse for intellectual activity. These conditions offer opportunities to decenter oneself, in other words, to step out of one's own perspective in order to consider the object of morality, which can be honesty, respect, honor, etc. From the intellectual understanding of this object, the action to be taken derives from the affective choice that the feeling of obligation imposes on the moral plane.

The ethical plane presupposes the moral plane, although the opposite is not true. La Taille (2006) points out that the concept of ethics answers the question "what life do I want to live?" This desired life includes the feeling of obligation in relation to the rules and the duty to comply with them. Thus, the "good life", from an ethical perspective, does not contradict moral rules. Although its psychological motivation is self-expansion, it is in conflict that the overcoming of self-esteem (understood as self-worth) by self-respect (self-worth, when one's actions follow moral values) is legitimized. In a conflictual situation, the choice that is made and the moral criteria that guide it may or may not conquer the ethical plane. For example, in a situation where finances are not going well, an account credit is mistakenly made by a certain company to a certain individual. [6]The word Moral comes from the Latin: *mores,* relating to customs.

If the beneficiary is aware of this fact and does not inform the responsible department that the credit was undue, the desire for financial gain does not outweigh the shame of facing up to dishonest conduct (i.e. self-respect is not lost).

Since, for Piaget, respect is the basis of morality, there is no way of practicing mutual respect if you are not worthy of respect. It's worth noting that, on the ëйec level, revealing undue credit indicates surrendering one's self-worth, because one is acting on the basis of a choice that privileges moral value (honesty) and that impacts on the "good life". However, if the honest attitude is motivated by the laurels that come from the honorable action, it is no longer a question of acting on the ëйec plane, because heteronomy prevails, which focuses on the other and on the reward, and not on the moral value in itself or on the self-respect that unites the moral plane with the ethical plane. It's not a question of "what will they think of me?"; on the contrary, the question is how can you "look in the mirror"? In fact, the ethical personality encompasses both the moral and ethical planes:

> Let's remember that we assume that the ethics of the feeling of

> obligation, essential to the moral plane, must be sought on the ёйот plane in the search for representations of oneself with positive value. Let's also remember that self-respect is the feeling that unites the moral and ethical planes, because it is, on the one hand, an expression of self-expansion - therefore an element of the "good life" - and, on the other hand, the essential cause of the feeling of obligation - therefore the motivation for moral action: he respects morality who, in doing so, respects himself. Therefore, moral development and the strengthening of the feeling of obligation that inspires it must be explained by the construction of an ethical personality (LA TAILLE, 2006, p. 133).

For Piaget (1932/1994), the moral coercion of the adult implies intellectual coercion. Thus, when we talk about autonomous morality, we are also talking about affective and cognitive development. It's possible to think that the heteronomous adult - who represents authority - contributes little to the development of autonomous morality in their pupils. Those who guide their choices and principles on the basis of what others think, judge or control, those who don't govern their own choices on the basis of what they believe and think is right, or who don't take them on, are unlikely to go beyond their stage of moral judgment. Phrases like "it's not my fault, I had no choice", "that's the system, what can I do?" or "what could I do? I'm obliged to obey" indicate, like so many others, a heteronomous morality. According to Lind (2000, p. 404), moral competence is "the bridge between good moral intentions and moral behavior". Hence its importance when thinking about the role of schools and their teachers in training students to be ethical citizens.

3.12 Justice: the view of theorists

John Rawls, an American philosopher, focused his thinking on the principles of a just and free society. In this sense, he built a theory of justice in which a social contract that established fair principles would be followed. For a just and free society, it is necessary to think about how to distribute goods and rights, and a convention with rules and principles would be needed to bring this idea to life. But who would produce these interest-free principles and rules? Society itself? In his book "A Theory of Justice" (RAWLS, 2000), he states that the principles of justice would be better established if it were possible to create a new social contract, which could only be created by someone using what he called the "voodoo of ignorance". The function of the "vdu" would be to preserve equity in the choice of the principles of justice, so that the contract would not be guided by distinctions in terms of social class, gender, religion, income, health, family, ethnicity, etc. The metaphor of the use of the stick therefore established the need for society to be guided by principles that ignored distinctions of skin color, gender, economic level, etc. The veil, therefore, would not allow any decision to be based on partiality, since ignorance would allow everyone to be in an equal position, resulting in a social contract free of personal interests (SANDEL, 2012), valid for all contracting parties.

According to Rawls (2000), the vacuum would ensure the creation of a fair contract, giving everyone respectful treatment, freedom and dignity, regardless of their situation or who they were. Equal treatment is, in this sense, desirable, because it is fair if everyone has the same opportunities, whether they are poor or rich, healthy or sick, male or female, etc.

The book "What is doing the right thing" (SANDEL, 2012) explains the idea of Rawls' new agreement or hypothetical social contract, by postulating the use of the "vow of ignorance":

> Rawls invites us to reason about the principles that we - as rational, self-interested people - would choose if we were in that position. He does not assume that we are all motivated only by self-interest in real life; he only asks us to put aside our moral and religious convictions in order to carry out this imaginary experiment. What principles would we choose? (SANDEL, 2012, p. 178).

However, the idea of the "vow of ignorance" seems to presuppose heteronomous subjects or, perhaps, those incapable of creating this social contract disinterested in personal privileges, in the name of equity. Although Rawls does not make this claim, it is worth reflecting on whether the "vdu" is equivalent to saying that only through a supposed situation of ignorance or lack of knowledge, called by Rawls (2000) the "original position", would it be possible to create conditions that would ensure fairness, because otherwise the contract would be partial. In this sense, subjects would be incapable of moral autonomy when it comes to constructing principles of justice.

For Rawls, the principle of the good is necessarily allied to justice, because they are complementary. Now, if it is desirable and just that a society's way of life preserves its rights to freedom, it is also true that ideas of the good cannot go beyond the limits of the just, the space authorized by justice. The good as rationality, from the same author's perspective (RAWLS, 2000), assumes that all citizens should be free and equal, and from this premise comes the first of two principles of justice.

The first principle of justice provides for a minimum of basic individual freedoms. Regardless of specific conceptions of the world (religious, philosophical, scientific), the good in this first principle of justice favors freedoms shared by all individuals, based on respect. The primary goods, as far as the principles of freedom are concerned, are considered in a brief list in "Justice and Democracy" (RAWLS, 2000) - freedom of movement, freedom to choose an occupation, freedom of expression, freedom of leisure, freedom to own property, freedom from physical pain, etc. - which are indispensable to a just society.

The second principle of justice refers to social and economic equity. Even so, it doesn't advocate that everyone be equal, favoring what it calls the principle of difference. Economic inequality is possible and acceptable, as long as the opportunities for the less advantaged are equal to those of the more economically or socially advantaged. Thus, the best school should be accessible to everyone, not just those who can afford it. Equal conditions of opportunity are a premise of this principle. In Brazil, for example, a young person who works all day and studies at night for the entrance exam would possibly have less chance of getting into a good university, compared to those whose parents can support them so that they only study. In this example, the second principle of justice would, for Rawls, be neglected, because it would be fair if the two young people could only study, but it would also be fair if, after the same opportunities, they achieved different positions, that is, one got into the best university and the other didn't, because given the same opportunities, justice was present.

Justice is conceived as fairness, without, however, being linked to utilitarian and generalized ideas. The definition of needs, however, is an elaborate political construction, mutually acceptable to the citizens and, for this reason, requires the "vow of ignorance" to create a social contract that serves everyone, without personal privileges. The good, in the principle of justice, praises just decisions and, in this way, people do not want what is good for them, but what is just for them, so there is a supremacy of the just over the good.

In an egalitarian society, the education of children primarily involves freedom of conscience, the study of civil and constitutional rights so that they become members capable of autonomy, respecting the equitable terms of social cooperation (RAWLS, 2000), which corroborates the ideas of Piaget, who treats cooperation as an essential element in society.

For Comte-Sponville (1999), virtue can be taught, unlike the Greek philosophy of Aristotle, where virtue is a natural gift, although he agrees with Aristotle that "virtue is what we are (and therefore what we can do)". In the book "Little Treatise on the Great Virtues", praising goodness, justice, courage, temperance, fortitude, gratitude, among many others, is intended to go against "[...] the morality of the sad and a sad morality." (COMTE-SPONVILLE, 1999, p. 4). Raising good morals, trying to understand what one should do and be, implies thinking about the other as well as oneself. In "sad morality", whining replaces virtue. It is in plurality that we become more human, that we really gain "human power" which, distinct from acquiring material things, makes us worthy precisely because we do good.

Like Rawls, Comte-Sponville criticizes utilitarianism[6] . What good is injustice to the majority? Could it be considered a good to cause harm to someone or to condemn an innocent person? No, that would be an ignominy. Justice refers to a greater good, which aims precisely to prohibit injustice, even if it benefits the collective (COMTE-SPONVILLE, 1999). There is no justification for injustice. In the name of feelings, would precious goods like love or happiness justify sacrificing someone? If that were the case, it would no longer be justice. From Comte-Sponville's perspective (1999), justice is based on both conformity to the law and equality. Social justice brings into discussion the great differences in economic resources, wealth and opportunities, which are not present in a just society. Conformity with the law, an aspect that also defines justice, refers only to legality that dialogues with and respects equality. Its inverse, according to Comte-Sponville (1999), runs counter to justice: "The just, inversely, is that which violates neither the law nor the legitimate interests of others, neither the law (in general) nor the rights (of individuals)." (p. 49). (p. 49). Thus, the law needs to be fair in order to ensure that individuals are equal before it, respecting their differences.

This first sense of justiga doesn't understand the law as synonymous with justiga, because if the law is unjust, it's fair to break it. Morality and justice come first, the law later, but ideally they should go hand in hand. The second meaning of justice refers to the concept of fairness, i.e. that there should be correspondence between individuals. However, it's not about the equivalent advantage for one side or the other, but rather that which, reciprocally, lives up to the symbol of the balance, because it doesn't favor either side: "[...] equity (from *aequus*, equal) is what would be synonymous with justice [...]" (COMTE-SPONVILLE, 1999, p. 52).

War, therefore, for the same author, cannot be just, because it is impossible for it to be, even if the rights and laws established seek to preserve some more than others, something that could perhaps be seen as partial justice which, even if it only serves some, would still be better than none at all. For example, a soldier or officer could be less unjust or more just in a decision, yet the situation of moral misery that is established in a war has no justice value. The indignity, pain, violence and so many other evils caused by battles are not, under any circumstances, just. For Comte-Sponville (1999), justice is an endless struggle that the just pursue in the name of equal rights and human dignity. In this struggle, unlike others, there is no room for injustice or evil, because it is a struggle without war, involved in the clear purpose

---

[6] Utilitarianism: a theory developed in English liberal philosophy, especially by Bentham (17481832) and Stuart Mill (1806-1873), which considers a good action or a good rule of conduct to be characterized by the utility and pleasure it can bring to an individual and, to an extent, to the community.

of re-establishing the ability to look beyond oneself.

Philosophy, therefore, praises justice as a greater good, a social necessity, based on the ability to see the other person as an end and not a means (KANT, 2003). Philosophers since ancient times have agreed that justice is a noble virtue, but who is responsible for instilling it in new generations? Not political ideology, because it offers guidelines that favor or repress values. A good example is the Nazi concentration camps which, based on the superiority of one race over the others, had very clear values, but fairness was certainly not one of them. The same was true of the Stalinist labor camps, where political prisoners or those who had committed crimes of theft, murder, rape, etc. were offered supposedly educational correction. Denial of food, exposure to the cold, forced labor and torture made up a value system under which millions of people suffered. Based on the Piagetian premise that morality is not an innate component, but a learned one, who is responsible for teaching it? How, where and who teaches justice? These are questions that have remained unanswered since antiquity.

Goergen (2007) points out the conflicts in society in relation to moral education. According to the author, there are disillusioned groups who don't believe in change or in moral education. There are those who feel too busy to think about it and the nostalgic, who miss the "good old days" when the rules were clear. Finally, the whiners and the accusers are also listed: they are the ones who, absolving themselves of responsibility, feel they are the victims of the faults committed by others.

The school, a social space dedicated to education, should have an important influence on the formation of children and young people through dialog. However, it is going through a crisis of values and confusion about its role in moral formation. The demands on the role of the school are confusing:

> [...] on the one hand, an education geared to the market, to competitiveness, to what is useful, and on the other, an education of the responsible, respectful, just moral subject. These two proposals are not only distinct, but to a large extent contradictory [...] (GOERGEN, 2007, p. 755).

The same author argues that freedom has a political character: the achievement of autonomy includes the ability to make decisions based not on the judgment of others, but on the ability to self-regulate, leading their way of thinking, feeling and acting in the most diverse circumstances in the social environment. In this sense, the school plays an important role, but the author points out another problematic issue: the lack of limits. Parental and school authority is constantly questioned by children and students, who demand equality with parents and teachers. Goergen (2007, p. 757) adds: "However, it is important to note that this crisis of authority and discipline also affects moral education, to the extent that the authority of the moral norm is questioned." He concludes that moral education, the discussion of values and the practice of those relating to justice, equality and respect is beyond the task of parents and teachers: it is the function of all public and private institutions: media, politics, law, etc. However, the school has a fundamental role to play in educating and practicing values, and it is up to it to undertake a major debate in favor of moral discernment, with an emphasis on justice.

For Piaget (1932/1994), justice is the most rational virtue, because the feeling of justice develops in children as solidarity and mutual respect are achieved and experienced in social relationships. This author's psychogeographic theory is also manifested in the proposal of the stages of cognitive development and moral life. For Piaget, there are three major periods in the development of justice, a construction that is not innate and occurs as a result of cognitive development, social experiences and the way in which the individual elaborates on all of this:

> There are three periods in the construction of the notion of justice. A period extending up to about the age of seven-eight, during which justice is subordinated to adult authority, a period between the ages of approximately eight and eleven, which is that of progressive egalitarianism and, finally, a period beginning around the age of eleven-twelve, during which justice is purely egalitarian and tempered by concerns for equity (PIAGET, 1932/1994, p. 236).

It should be noted that children's notion of justice is directly linked to their perceptions of sanctions. According to Piaget's research (1932/1994), children of different ages judged whether the punishments presented in short stories were fair or which ones were fairer. It was on the basis of the children's responses that the periods mentioned above were established. With regard to sanctions, Piaget mentions three types of justice: distributive justice, which is defined by equality and is manifested in reciprocal sanctions; retributive justice, which is defined by the proportionality of the act in relation to the sanction, found in both reciprocal and expiatory sanctions; and finally, immanent justice, which is considered to come from the actions themselves.

Immanent justice can be seen in examples such as the small child who kicks the chair he has tripped over, as if the chair were to blame, or the older child who steals a sweet from the bakery and, as it has fallen into the sewer, attributes the immorality of his action to the falling sweet. It would be pertinent for the person who considers the thesis of immanent justice to justify that the candy fell because it was stolen, because if it had been bought, it certainly wouldn't have fallen into the sewer. In adults, divine punishments are good examples of immanent justice.

In retributive justice, a sanction is unjust when it punishes an innocent person or rewards a guilty one, or when it doesn't balance the merit and the reward, or the fault and the punishment. Distributive justice implies the idea of equal rights and duties, and concerns the application of laws to a group of subjects. In this case, injustice occurs when some people are favored at the expense of others. In the concept of distributive justice, fairness is not restricted to conceiving the law as equal for all, but to considering the circumstances in which it occurs, taking into account different factors.

4 METHOD

4.1 Objective

The aim of this research is to analyze what students between the ages of 13 and 18, who are trying to improve their basic education in order to enter the job market, say about the values of justice.

It's common to hear that moral values are in crisis, that children and young people have no limits and that a lot has been lost from the education of yesteryear, when the mere sight of parents would inhibit a child's possible inappropriate behavior. In view of this initial finding, the research aims to listen to and deepen young people's understanding of moral values, in particular justice.

Knowing what young people say, the ideas they defend and the moral values they highlight, can offer good possibilities for analysis and, perhaps, educational programs aimed at such discussions and space to share ideas about moral values.

4.2 The Institution

The data was collected at a non-formal educational institution whose aim is to offer students opportunities to improve on the formal education they received in public primary and secondary schools. Classes are held at the institution on weekends, in a variety of courses: English, administrative assistance, mechanics, capoeira, guitar, adult literacy, professional initiation and newspaper project, among others, lasting one or two semesters.

The institution runs courses for children, young people and adults in a suburb in the south of the city of Sao Paulo. The classrooms have collective tables, which encourages interaction between students, a blackboard and a projector, which can be requested for classes. For this research, the institution provided a classroom and the participants sat at desks arranged in a circle.

4.3 Subjects

The subjects are 7 students from the institution who agreed to take part in a focus group to talk about justice. The number of 7 students is part of the guidelines for forming the focus group, which in smaller numbers, or more than 10 participants, can limit everyone's participation and the opportunity to exchange ideas.

All the young people have voluntarily signed up for the courses they are taking at the non-formal institution, in order to further their studies and think about entering the job market.

The study was explained to them, as well as the need to sign an informed consent form, making it clear that they were guaranteed the right to keep their identity and that of the institution confidential, as well as the possibility of leaving the study at any time.

According to Gatti (2012), the selection of participants needs to follow certain criteria that make it possible to pursue the research problem and qualify them based on common characteristics for the collection of analytical material. For this research, we established characteristics of these young people that met the two main behaviors observed by the institution that nominated them. For the focus group, these behaviors would be vitally important, since without them the material collected would possibly not meet the research objective. The selection criteria were:

1. Easy to express opinions, presenting his points of view and his personal daily experiences;
2. Being able to listen to your colleagues and keep the debate going.

Gender was also determined and a balanced number of men and women were chosen. This division was made with the aim of collecting the ideas of both genders and then analyzing whether there is a difference in the arguments used to defend one moral value or another and whether there is a gender implication in their positions.

Piaget and Kohlberg's studies on morality did not differentiate between the morality of men and women; cognition is what runs through this theory, regardless of gender. Although there was a wide range of content indicators from other studies, such as moral competence (LIND, 2000), the gender distinction was not achieved. Carol Gilligan (1982), however, brought up the "ethics of generosity and care", presenting the idea that there is a different way for women to reason, that there is a "voice" that needs to be heard and that indicates other perspectives related to concern for relationships, for example, which justify their moral judgments. The "different voice" referred to by Gilligan (1982) is the voice of care, different from the male voice, the "voice" of justice, as opposed to the female voice.

Conveniently, all the young people taking part in the research live in the same peripheral neighborhood in the south of Sao Paulo, and all are public school students who have completed, or have already completed, high school. According to Gatti (2012), the regularity of the focus group must meet the objective of the research. In order to collect data on what young people think about the moral value of justice, the equivalent socio-economic condition can favor free debate, and this homogeneity "can facilitate the development of intra-group communication." (GATTI, 2012, p. 19), since class or other conflicts can generate friction that interferes with the exchange on the topic proposed in the research, even though different opinions are desirable.

The focus group maintains an open atmosphere for discussion, promoted by the facilitator so that the participants feel confident in presenting their opinions voluntarily. However, there is no need to prepare them beforehand, as the aim is to bring out specific questions about the proposed topic (GATTI, 2012).

4.4 Procedures

Data was collected using the focus group technique, in the institution itself, lasting one hour and fifty minutes, with the researcher mediating.

Before the discussion began, the mediator confirmed the duration, guaranteed identity confidentiality and permission not to stay. The participants were informed of the routine of the meeting and what was expected of them, which was to be an open conversation, with no judgment of right or wrong regarding opinions, nor was consensus expected. They wanted debate and respect for ideas that differed from their own. A badge was provided to identify the interlocutor, which contributed to the transcription of the speeches.

The mediator explained at the beginning his role of introducing the subject, proposing questions, listening and helping everyone to express themselves and ensuring that the subject is kept to, thus avoiding rehashing such points during the discussions (GATTI, 2012).

The initial instructions included an invitation for participants to write down what they understand by justice. They could put down concepts, examples and ideas to think about before the discussion began.

The participants were invited to say what they thought about the subject. After their comments on justice, some critical episodes were presented by the moderator based on the questions posed by the group, so that everyone could give their opinion, using the trigger: what seems fair to you?

The judge's dilemma is part of the *Moral Judgment Test* (MJT), created by Georg Lind

(2000) and translated by Bataglia, Moraes and Lepre (2010).

Everyone signed an informed consent form. The conversation during the focus group was filmed, recorded and transcribed. The film allows the speech of each participant to be identified. After re-reading the transcribed material, the students' responses were analyzed. Categories of responses were constructed a posteriori.

The data was analyzed qualitatively, so that the content presented by the participants could be analyzed. Based on the ideas expressed about justice, injustice and other values that may permeate the arguments, the data could be categorized by similarity, in cases where identical values, such as honesty, appear as a justification for an attitude considered just.

4.5 Analysis benchmark

The data collected through the focus group was transcribed, including laughter, intonation (volume of voice, pauses, euphoria) and the researcher's interventions, which should be restricted to repeating what the young people said, either to confirm their ideas or to better understand the various points of view. We then tried to establish a posteriori categories, which were discussed in the light of Jean Piaget's psychogendic theory and also those of other authors studied who deal with moral judgment.

5 DATA ANALYSIS AND DISCUSSION

"As long as laws are necessary, men are not capable of freedom."
Pythagoras.

This chapter discusses the data collected through the focus group, in which the young people discussed the topic of Justice. The critical episodes contributed to triggering the conversations, giving rise to disagreements, consents, changes of mind and, in general, complements to what their colleagues were saying. After listening to and re-reading the young people's speeches many times, four categories and subcategories were created in order to organize the content found. The themes that stood out and named the categories were all based on the idea of justice and injustice, such as: the school, the principal and his educational character, laws, sanctions and discrimination. Table 1 shows the categories and subcategories:

Table 1 - Categories constructed a posteriori and their subcategories.

Categories	Sub-categories
School	The school's educational role: dialogue
	The role of the head teacher
	Study as a means to a future
	Indiscipline
Laws	The responsibilities of the authorities and the
	Equality
Sangoes	By reciprocity
	Atonements
Discrimination	Socioeconomics

Source: The author (2016).

5.1 The School

For young people, school seems to be a fertile ground for moral learning. Teachers and principals occupy a central place in this issue, which highlights the role of these adults' attitudes in the daily lives of teenagers. They are not only responsible for providing good examples that will shape the students' education, but also for being the shapers of moral conduct. In fact, morality can be defined as the collection of established rules that guide duty towards others (TOGNETTA, 2009), which is necessary for an ethical personality. In the words of the young people, the school teaches rules, which should be done by demanding a student's attitude, sanctions, the way classes are taught and, above all, the way they interfere in interpersonal relationships. All these aspects, in harmony with the young people, contribute to their formation, leading them to achieve self-regulation.

5.1.1 The school's educational role: dialogue

Goergen (2007), as already mentioned, reveals a panorama full of conflicts in moral education, among them those posed by the "nostalgists", who see the current moment as chaos compared to past times, as if today's young people were uninterested in education and especially moral education. The group's account reveals not only concern about the school environment, but also about the image of the institution. They criticize violence, the negligence of some schools with regard to their educational role, and also have concerns about what their parents will think of their school in the face of scenes they consider immoral. They repeat phrases like "what will they think, what kind of school is this?"

Imagine what the parents, the other students, will come home and say: "Mom, I was at school, then I came home, got into a fight, pulled my hair, screamed..." What will that mom think?

(Giba, 18)

Parents will think "what school is that?".

(Maria, 16)

I come home (and say): "It was a shambles, you don't understand".

(Luca, 15)

Parents will think, "What kind of school is this? What structure is the school giving my child?".

(Mary, 16)

It seems that the young people point out that, in their family group, school is seen as a training ground that has an influence and impact on the students, contradicting the often-heard complaints that the current generation has few prospects in life. When given a voice, the opposite is observed: teenagers seem to value school and expect it to be a fair and learning environment. In the same way, they value dialogue, because they want to be heard and believe they need to listen. In their speeches, "I want to be heard, but it's only fair that I listen too" appeared, directly or indirectly. As Piaget (1977) points out, authoritarianism exerts moral and intellectual coercion, while dialog and cooperation contribute to the autonomous formation of young people. This seems to be a common understanding among the research participants:

I think it should be like this in all schools and not just anything being... suspended. It's not like that, there has to be a dialog.

(Maria, 16)

A lot of this (ethical learning) is missing and it's not worked on when you're young. That's missing a lot... At the school where I practically spent my childhood, they worked a lot on the value of ethics. I read so many books on ethics that, my God, to do the summaries, I ended up thinking "man, it makes sense". It has to make sense, because we live with people. In any case, we can't please everyone, but having common sense means that this doesn't happen and this issue of ethics, common sense, etc., is very rarely dealt with in schools. That's the formation of young people, you spend your life there.

(Giba, 18)

Reciprocal sanctions (PIAGET, 1932/1994), even though they are rarely experienced by young people, seem to be a desire to be achieved. We sometimes see voices that contradict each other, in which dialogue is either useless or needs to be practiced and taught. In this sense, they choose the adult to direct this path. They value being heard and listening, an important component of life in society. Another contradictory aspect of the participants' speech refers to the role of punishment, seen as important to curb inappropriate actions. In short, the group investigated wants an ethical environment, marked by the presence of rules and dialog, and there is some agreement that punishment is important. The value placed on this last aspect suggests that young people's behavior is marked by heteronomy, which places the permission to act in one way or another in the hands of the adult. Giba, when reporting on the reading of ethics books, pointed out that this was given to him as a punishment at school and, even though it didn't hurt him, punishing instead of solving problems only maintains moral heteronomy. Dialogue is an important resource for children and young people to become unbalanced and decentered, and Giba's speech was endorsed with euphoria by young people who believed that educational work on ethics in relationships was precarious.

5.1.2 The role of the head teacher

According to Piaget (1932/1994), children are initially heteronomous due to their cognitive condition. Autonomy, although it is a long process full of cognitive conflicts, is made possible by both the cognitive stage and the affective constructions developed by the child or young person. It is not, therefore, a natural consequence, but rather an elaboration that takes place through a series of physical and social experiences and also through biological maturation. In this sense, the authority figure is central for young people to achieve moral autonomy. Children with concrete operative thinking, and even later with formal thinking, need adults to help them go beyond their point of view. Parents, teachers and principals have a great responsibility, as Tognetta (2009) points out: "The role that adults play in introducing children and adolescents to the world of morality is essential." (p. 95). In childhood, the adult exercises power over the child and is, for them, the moral reference who teaches them to respect the rules, because at this age they are not able to distinguish between what is appropriate and what is inappropriate, a function that falls to the adult, who establishes a relationship of unilateral respect with the children. Then, with older children and adolescents, it is expected that there will be an evolution from unilateral respect to mutual respect, in which the authority figure helps the process of decentralization, i.e. helps them to understand that rules go far beyond obedience, since they are intended to maintain relationships. In this way, children and young people learn to consider others and move towards moral autonomy.

The young people pointed out their indignation when reporting scenes of their school's principal, saying that it wasn't fair for her to hold such a position. Also, because they don't admire this professional, they don't legitimize the sanctions she applies:

I think it depends on how you punish and who the principal is. For example, at my school, the principal, one of the times there was a disagreement, I went to the principal' office, I went into the room, there's a TV, a fridge and a sofa. And I was like, "What is this woman doing here, people?". I went in, she was in her room, and she looked in and... she said that I didn't have the right to do such a thing, that everyone was wrong, she'd suspend me and call the parents, that's it. She wasn't even interested in the case. In other words, (we) arrive and she doesn't want to know what happened, she's going to give the punishment that's already standardized for everyone who's going to be there... She'll only look into the situation if the parents come.
Because otherwise there won't be any. Then you imagine: I want to talk to the principal, she's busy, but you open the door and she's lying down...

(Luca, 15)

But that's always the case.

(Ruth, 16)

This has already happened at school. A mother came in and opened the classroom and she was there, lying down...

(Luca, 15)

Piaget (1977), in presenting his ideas on education, reinforces the value of respect as essential for the formation of moral conscience. Respect, a mixture of love and fear in heteronomy, is replaced, in autonomy, by fear of decaying in the eyes of others. It is in this sense that admiration is fundamental to this achievement. La Taille (2006) points out that losing prestige for someone you don't admire and respect is of little help to the moral conscience. The young people's discussion of the principal's attitude reveals precisely this: that the principal's clumsiness is harmful to the educational process. For young people, it can be more difficult to understand and practice justice when they feel wronged by the person who is the highest authority in the school. If they don't trust the principal's judgment in everyday situations, there's no way for them to make judgments among themselves that consider different perspectives and solutions to the same problem.

5.1.3 Study as a means to a future

For young people, study and schooling seem to represent an important opportunity to "be something in life". They say that a person needs to study in order to be admirable and therefore have a role in society. In this way, school is, in the view of the survey participants, a means of achieving material success and social prestige. Although this is a widely held notion, school is not understood in its role of forming citizens, which involves teaching content, procedures and also attitudes and values. Rawls (2000) sees education as a fundamental aspect of an egalitarian society, which includes freedom of conscience and the expected autonomy. This point of view can be seen in the students' responses to episode 2, in which a young student had given up her room to a family member and this had jeopardized her studies:

Because she (the student) is studying to have a future.

(Luca, 15)

Because, as he said, her (the student's) future is at stake, she needs to study, she needs to qualify and it's one of the most important stages in a teenager's life.

(Bela, 18)

In addition to attending school and having already completed some of the stages of basic education, the participants in this study showed that they value what is learned at school, the cultural and intellectual baggage that is built up there. They pointed out that not taking advantage of their classes would be a detriment to them and, consequently, would mean fewer opportunities in the future:

It's very unethical of you (to say): "here's the test, I'm going to charge you..." Well, you're a student, it's your duty to study. And who's going to take the test, see the answers and learn what? Nothing. "I outsmarted the teacher, that's great", then you get to the third year... "Did you study that?", "I did", "Can you do it?", "No".
(Giba, 18)

Although the young people were indignant about the unethical attitude of principals and teachers, they also criticized those who don't assume their responsibilities as students:

(Why don't they know?) "Because the teacher didn't teach them". That's usually what they say.
(Luca, 15)

And the excuse.
(Giba, 18)

The teacher will have nothing to do with his grade.
(Joice, 17)

The money will still be in my account... The teacher speaks. Whether I learn or not.

(Ruth, 16)

5.1.4 Indiscipline

As Devries and Zan (1998) refer to the socio-moral environment, whether or not the school intends to invest in students' moral development, it does so through a parallel, impersonal curriculum. Young people are also observant of their peers and the desires they express in terms of participation and involvement with the school's proposals. If they sometimes judge the school to be inadequate and uncommitted to its educational task, they also do so when reporting on the behavior of some students. According to the students, some of their colleagues' attitudes are also seen as inappropriate at school and unfair to those who want to learn. In fact, it is clear from what they say that they feel aggrieved by the climate caused by disinterest, rowdiness and anger in the classroom. They even expect the school to take a stand and take appropriate measures to guarantee their right to learn, while respecting others.

The truth is that the vast majority of students today want nothing to do with anything. If there's a conference in every room of forty students, ten to twenty at most want something.

(Luca, 15)

There was a girl in my class who always fought; she'd say: "I'm going to fight today, because I'm going to be suspended, I'm going to stay at home for two days, I won't have to come to school". She said it like that.

(Bela, 18)

Taking suspension to them is very good.

(Luca, 15)

(laughs) Getting suspended for staying at home?

(Ruth, 16)

5.2 Laws

One of the findings of this study relates to how young people associate justice with obeying the law. Colby and Kohlberg (1987) point out that children only gradually build up their worldview and morals. Biaggio (2006) mentions an article written by Kohlberg (1968 apud BIAGGIO, 2006) - "The child as a moral philosopher" - in which the author explains how, through social relationships and cognitive maturation, children move from one stage to another, larger and more comprehensive than the previous one, until they reach moral autonomy. Colby and Kohlberg (1987) established stages in the development of moral reasoning, based on Piaget's psychogendic theory, something that can be identified in young people's talk about laws, the obligation to comply with them and the importance of maintaining social order.

5.2.1 The responsibilities of the authorities and the public

The discussion about laws arose from one of the critical episodes presented (episode 1). When discussing the judge's decision (to torture a suspect), they stressed the importance of everyone following the law, otherwise the world would be in chaos. Initially, most of the young people agreed with the fact that the law is above all else, that it is indisputable and that it offers the population greater security, since it spells out what and how people are expected to act. However, in the course of the debate, some young people changed their position and began to question the law: if it serves people, then it can't be superior to their needs and rights. Although they thought about it, none of the young people considered the possibility of the law being changed or the law being unfair. The focus group effectively allowed reflection on ideas, facts and circumstances, with a possible change of opinion. As evidenced in and through the dialog, opinions and beliefs are rethought and replaced by others:

And as the judge, the highest authority, he should follow the law. If it's forbidden, why is he doing it? Why is he allowing it? Not to mention that he can't save other people's lives [...]. A person mistreating a person...

(Joice, 17)

What if that person is innocent? Not guilty?
(Beto, 13)

And even if she is guilty, she can't.

***(Joice**, 17)*

And against the law.
(Ruth, 16)

Law and law.

(Maria, 16)

If he's the judge, he can't do that, because it's in the law.
(Beto, 13)

By making these statements, it is possible to infer the level of moral judgment called by Colby and Kohlberg (1987) stage 4, or "conventional", which refers to the possibility of the individual recognizing the other person's perspective and respecting the social order, as well as the authority of the judge. At this stage, the figure of the other is already taken into account, although the possibility of changing the law when it overrides the needs of the individual is not yet considered. This perspective, however, only appears in the next stage of moral judgment: the "post-conventional" stage.

However, Bela's speech is autonomous (although in other speeches it is heteronomous), revealing her ability to decentralize and attribute responsibility for her actions and the maintenance of social relations to everyone. Bela seems to see beyond her own perspective, when she criticizes those who attribute total responsibility for justice or for maintaining society's rights to the government (or to others).

Justiga was, for me, a name given to people so that they would settle down and think that, for example, the government has a duty to help and they don't. If you see a homeless person, for example, you're not going to stop and ask them if they're thirsty, hungry. If you see a homeless person, for example, you're not going to stop and ask them if they're thirsty or hungry, because you think it's the government's duty. I think we should get together to help these people, because it's only fair. We have (food) and we should also want to give people that.

(Bela, 18)

5.2.2 Equality

The idea of equality also featured prominently in discussions about justice. The young people seem to want everyone to have the same financial situation, the same opportunities and the same rights, something that reminds us of the concept of corrective justice postulated by Aristotle. In the words of the young people, it is fair to establish the same rights and duties through the law, ignoring the particular needs of each person, as if they believed that what they thought was right would possibly be accepted by everyone. This is heteronomous thinking, albeit in compromise, as some comments and reticence suggest:

I don't think justice exists in the world we live in. Because for me, justice is doing the right thing and giving people equal rights. But that doesn't exist.

(Bela, 18) *For me, justice and equality is a basic right for all citizens. But here in Brazil, especially, there's a lot of inequality and, I think, especially among the lower classes, the poor, and prejudice is a factor... a lot of inequality. I think it's also fair to follow the laws.*

(Joice, 17)

These opinions seemed to be anchored in painful personal experiences, so that disentangling oneself is still a challenge when young people talk about the law and equality:

Well, my concept of justice is basically what they've already said: equality, above all. Like, for example, I think there should be no social class, that everyone should have the same income, everyone should have a house.

(Luca, 15)

When the two girls spoke about whether the judge's decision to torture the suspect was fair (or not), the others nodded, looked at each other and said quietly: "And...", "It could be", as if they were expanding on their previously held ideas about justice. From Joice and Ruth's perspective, the person who was being suspected also deserved to have their rights preserved, a situation that was not initially considered in the conversation.

But if justice is equality, he (the judge) has to guarantee equality for both parties. Even if it's proven that she is or isn't. He has to guarantee it for both parties, both for the people who are innocent and for her, who is a criminal. It's equality: you can't say that you can mistreat her because she's committed a crime, because she's a suspect...

(Joice, 17)

There's a point that talks about saving all lives... He (the judge) won't be saving all lives if he accepts and tortures the woman. Her life will be harmed. So that point is wrong.

(Ruth, 16)

Another finding in this study comes close to what was proposed by Rawls (2000), when he believes that, in equality, everyone should have the same rights. According to the author, no one should be privileged, as everyone is under the same social contract and subject to the same laws. Rute and Joice thus seem to agree with the principle of equality.

5.3 Sangoes

When dealing with sanctions, it is possible to highlight two sub-themes: limits and conflicts. Piaget (1932/1994) sees conflict as necessary for development. In this sense, when an individual or interpersonal conflict arises, the individual needs to look for ways to resolve it, a process that causes the cognitive disorganization necessary for new mental adaptations to lead the subject to rebalance themselves, through actions that solve the problem. In this way, conflict is a fundamental mechanism for the development of intelligence. It's worth pointing out that mental rebalancing to resolve the conflict doesn't mean making moral decisions, since mental processes can (or can't) produce actions aimed at oneself or others which, in the moral sphere, depend on the learning already explained above. In interpersonal relationships, conflicts often generate the need for sanctions. In democratic environments, sanctions for reciprocity predominate and, in general, coercive and authoritarian environments generate expiatory sanctions.

Boundaries are commonly interpreted as part of education, as ways of presenting rules, whether to children or students. Boundaries exist to demarcate physical territories or those that occur on the level of relationships, so that crossing them can be seen as an infringement. In such cases, the sanctions are to respect the territory that the boundaries establish. However, crossing boundaries can be seen as something positive and necessary when it comes to breaking rules that are considered unjust. Peacefully accepting a boundary that provides for non-intervention when a father assaults his son, thinking that it is not appropriate to cross the family boundary, is to cower in the face of injustice.

In fact, they are two sides of the same coin: often, it's the same person who doesn't cross the boundaries to be overcome and who crosses those to be respected. (LA TAILLE, 2000 p. 51).

Sanctions, therefore, need to take into account not only respect for limits, but also their transposition.

5.3.1 By reciprocity

For the focus group participants, sanction through reciprocity seemed to be something that was still far from their reality. Making up for a mistake, without suffering punishment or any kind of psychological or physical pain, is still not something they consider. Episode 3, which dealt with a punishment given by a school principal for physical aggression between two girls, was the scene that provoked the most discussion among the participants. The young people seemed motivated to give their examples and ideas, and yet there was less talk of reciprocal sanctions than expiatory ones. Physical aggression was considered by the young people to be very inappropriate, while verbal aggression was less prominent, even though it took place in the same context.

Being hit is not a punishment, it is aggression, violence.

(Joice, 17)

It's because many people believe that dialogue doesn't work. I went to a school from the first to the eighth grade that was all about dialog. Only if you extrapolated. I've done a lot of things that, my God... Only if I went so far over the limit that there was no way out, that the management would say: "you've gone beyond the limit of what's the limit...", because there must be several limit barriers; I think I broke three of them. Anyway, they would sit down and talk. And they did a lot of this psychological stuff. They showed you that you were wrong, that you had made a mistake. They didn't come in with "you're wrong!", call the father "you're wrong!". No. They would sit down, talk to you, in short, there was all this.

(Giba, 18)

They think that expulsion is the right punishment. No. They have to have a dialogue, say it's not right...

(Ruth, 16)

Although the speeches were controversial during the subsequent debates, as they sometimes defended dialogue and sometimes affirmed the need to punish those who made mistakes, they seemed to agree at the time with Giba's statement about the need for dialogue, as it was the best method of solving problems. This is an opportunity to articulate different points of view. By recognizing the other person's understanding of a given conflict situation, it is necessary to put oneself in the other person's shoes, which is a fundamental aspect of solving problems through sanction by reciprocity.

Taking the other person's point of view into account, decentering oneself, requires reflecting on one's own actions and being able to judge them beyond one's own point of view. This is a cognitive exercise that moves towards moral autonomy, so it is a key factor in establishing a cooperative environment. Luca and Joice discussed the disciplinary means that could be used to promote reflection on the problem and, consequently, repair the error.

Do you have to stop and think, or are you the one in the wrong? You have to care about yourself and not about who is punishing you, because if you're wrong, it's your fault.

(Luca, 15)

But it's a physical pain (referring to the girl in episode 3 who was assaulted), it's not going to get better. The person just won't want to do it because they'll hurt themselves later. It's not the same as reading a book, which will work on the person's mind. Maybe they'll come out of it learning something. Learning about an author, appreciating a book, something, will bring about a mental evolution. It's different.

(Joice, 17)

The right thing to do would be for him to hear both points, both people, and that of an outsider who is accompanying them. Because, often, the person favors themselves by telling their story. So he would need a witness who was neither a friend of one nor a friend of the other. It would be a stalemate.

(Luca, 15)

The dialog and the interventions from an adult showed the way of thinking of the young people, who considered that authority figures needed to play an educational role and mediate conflicts. This suggests that the participants still had difficulties in making decisions and remained intemperate. Depending on how they are treated, they will act fairly or unfairly in interpersonal relationships. Vinha's (2000) warning that "most adults need to police and train themselves in order to be able to react to incidents and clumsiness in a constructive way" is very apt. (p. 283).

Despite the prominence of the dialogue and the condemnation of some punishments, a debate between Maria and Luca opened up space for a new reflection, which caused the other participants to doubt which position to take. At times they seemed to agree with the statements made by the two people involved, albeit in contradictory ways. For Maria, in particular, it was the mother and then the father who had the legitimacy to choose the type of punishment to be given to their children, without relating it to morality, since, for her, the parents' decision is absolute and unquestionable, due to the role they occupy. According to Gilligan (1982), in "A different voice", there is a distinction between female and male ethics. For the author, depending on the issue under debate, unlike Colby and Kohlberg's (1987) assertions, there is a capacity for men and women to change their opinions considering the conflict at hand. For the same author, women's way of reasoning is different, given that the "ethics of care and generosity" play a central role. However, the participant's speech reveals that any action taken by the mother is fair, as it is mobilized by care and love. In this way, Maria seems to justify any and all actions that come from mothers, including violent ones. Luca, on the other hand, seems to defend the sanction of reciprocity.

I think... One: it's fair, yes, that of the family. Because it was your family who put you into the world, so they can beat you, they can take your life, as my mother says...

(Maria, 16)

I think that's wrong.

(Luca, 15)

Now, someone else who didn't put you in the world or anything, comes and wants to kill you, beat you up, it's not fair.

(Maria, 16)

I think you're wrong about that, because there are many families where people are aggressive for no reason. The person is stressed, they're going to de-stress by doing this. It's not right for you to say that (if) it's in the family, then it's OK to hit. I think it's wrong anyway.

(Luca, 15)

5.3.2 Atonements

Punishment as a strategy for correcting mistakes, and thus as a disciplinary measure, seems to be an everyday social issue, justified by the current problem of non-compliance with rules and thus with morals. Through the young people's speeches, it was possible to perceive a certain imitation of adult discourse, since in their speeches they appeared: "as my grandmother says", "my father" or "my mother". This reproduction of speeches seemed to have in common the social agreement that punishment is a good educational resource for children and young people. Some statements legitimized punishment as a corrective measure:

Just like Super Nanny does: she sits in the discipline corner. Because whether she likes it or not, they're young people; young people only learn when they're punished. I had to have several punishments, not physical, but kind of psychological, like "if you do this, this will happen to you, and for you to think about it, you'll stay in your house for three days". Young people, unfortunately, only learn when they're shocked, whether they want to be or not...

(Giba, 18) I agree with that, yes. You should really be punished, because... First of all, taking a photo in a bikini, what's the need? (Referring to episode 3) And then sending it to your friend's boyfriend? There's no need. It's very obvious, she should be beaten up. I completely agree: you have to give a suspension, even more so on exam day, so that you have the link that you'll never do it again. That's it.
(Maria, 16)

It's not fair that she should have this psychological pressure, but what she did was wrong. She has to be punished somehow.
(Giba, 18)

I think the board should take some action. Some attitude. Either suspension or expulsion...
(Beto, 13)

If, instead of staying at home, you stayed at school for longer, maybe it would have more effect than staying at home. Staying longer would be a better punishment.
(Bela, 18)

For some young people, the more severe the punishments, or the more discomfort they cause, the better their educational effect. Tiba (2007), commenting on the formation of ethical citizens, emphasizes the importance of children and young people being respected so that they can be respected. The author defends the importance of setting limits and gives guidance on how to do this. When discussing the "three styles of acting", he talks about "animal-style behavior", which is revealed in the attitude of adults when they "don't use rationality; they always repeat the same mistakes; they use the law of the strongest". (TIBA, 2007, p. 82). These attitudes don't give young people the chance to reflect on their mistakes and how to make amends. They often use their intelligence to escape punishment.

(the punishment) Fair enough, of course it is. But not for me...
(Maria, 16)

We're saying this (about the punishment being appropriate), but in this case, if we were, we'd say "I don't want to".
(Luca, 15)

No, that's absurd (referring to her receiving a punishment, but not applying it to the other person)... You would revolt.
(Maria, 16)

The speeches reveal that even though the participants think the punishments are fair, they try to cheat them in order to avoid suffering. The fact that "punishment is fair, but not for you" seems to indicate a difficulty for young people to understand the consequences of their actions. In general, this happens when they don't participate in the construction of the rules and therefore don't reflect on them. In addition, they don't learn to dialog, to identify their pros and cons, so they become alien to their understanding and validation. Heteronomy is maintained in this context.

Vinha (2000) argues that the cooperative environment takes place in day-to-day relationships, which vary "[...] whether they are democratic (based on mutual respect) or authoritarian (based on unilateral respect)". (p. 394). Without offering children and young people a certain amount of freedom to govern themselves, the authoritarian relationship is maintained, in which the student obeys and the adult determines punishments and pain. There will thus be a chasm to cross in order to achieve moral autonomy and practice cooperation. It is a great mistake to assume that, with the passage of time and advancing age, moral autonomy will be achieved, as the results of research by Piaget (1932/1994) and Colby and Kohlberg (1987) clearly refute.

5.4 Discrimination

The concept of equality permeates the different discourses on justice, from Philosophy to Law and Psychology. Equality of basic rights, as explained by Rawls (2000) and equality as a presupposition of distributive justice, according to Piaget (1932/1994), are two examples of the fact that equality is always desired by human beings. It's possible to say that no one would appreciate or consider it fair to be the victim of exclusions while the other enjoys privileges. This seems to be a point on which there is no disagreement.

Although justice is recognized, it is injustice that recurs in human history. Indigenous Brazilians were and still are massacred, disrespected and expelled from their land; blacks had their human rights violated by slavery. These and countless other stories confirm humanity's difficulty in dealing with equality. Discrimination, which leads to prejudice, reveals a difficulty in self-regulation, a difficulty in recognizing rights and, therefore, a difficulty in recognizing and accepting the greater virtue of justice. Identifying defects and deficiencies in others, and acting with disrespect and discrimination, reveals heteronomous morality, lacking the ability to be moved, to move towards generosity (TOGNETTA, 2003), a virtue that is equally essential in a just society.

5.4.1 Socio-economic and ethnic discrimination

Indignation seemed to be present in the young people's speech when they were asked what they considered to be justice, apparently linked to a moral content, made up of negative emotions close to anger and expressed by demands and complaints, generally in a serious and convinced tone. The relationship with morality is explained by the general indignation when it comes to hurting rights and committing injustices. Economic inequalities, in particular, were reported in a louder tone of voice, sometimes interrupted by the others, who nodded with phrases like: "it's absurd", "only in this country", "wow!". The research participants live in a peripheral neighborhood with a high crime rate, so their speeches showed their anger at the socio-economic situation and the injustices that result from it.

So when you go to court and there's a person who has more resources, a rich person, and a lower-middle class person, surely the rich person is more favored.

(Joice, 17)

There's a lot of inequality in these parts, because... for me, what's right for one is right for all. And many people do it totally differently, because some people think they're rich, they think they're top, they think they have a lot and they have nothing, they think they can do everything, and that's not the case. I think that no matter how humble or poor a person is, they should also have the right to everything that rich people have. I think that's it.

(Maria, 16)

In treatments of inequality, devaluation occurs in the comparison, attributing greater value to one individual than to another. Self-judgment, in these circumstances, is negative, because a young person who says they are in a situation of injustice and discrimination because of their socio-economic condition, can feel humiliated and victimized by a social condition that doesn't give them opportunities. On the other hand, the feeling of indignation and demand can mobilize these young people to fight for justice, so that nonconformity can be a spring that drives necessary social change.

La Taille (2006) talks about the feeling of shame, in the moral sense, linked to the "self", which manifests itself in negative self-judgment. You feel ashamed of your bad image, when you fall down in your own eyes or in the eyes of others. In the following story, one of the young people presents a scene in which his group of friends wanted to leave a place because they feared unjust reprisals from the locals. When he explained the situation, he realized that the group's self-image was negative, because they saw themselves as people who couldn't even stay on the street, even if they were just chatting, because they could be taken by criminals.

Just like me the other day. I was near the school, I'd just left the student union, and the police started staring. People started to get scared and I said: "No, you don't need to be scared because you haven't done anything, you're just here, we were rehearsing what we were going to say in each class.". For me, justice doesn't exist in Brazil.

(Beto, 13)

The discrimination they suffer seems to generate in young people the same feeling of which they are victims: prejudice. They talk about those with high purchasing power, or white people, as being to blame for their condition, revealing that the socio-moral environment in which they live has a strong influence on the construction of their values.

So, Justice, I think it serves to bring order to society, but this order isn't so clear, because people are very prejudiced. For example, if a policeman sees a group of young people, sitting there, doing nothing, they're not doing anything, if they're of Luca's color (blacks specifically), the policeman will tell them to stop, put them against the wall and, if they say anything, they'll be beaten up and they've done nothing wrong. Now, if they see a group of whites, daddy's boys, rich people, and these rich people are doing something wrong, drinking, smoking, they don't do anything, they just pass by. This is injustice on the part of the government, even more so because of the corrupt police force we have today.

(Ruth, 16)

It's worth mentioning that schools and public policies play an important role in young people's helplessness, as inequality has negative consequences for moral development, whether it leads to blind conformism or revolt (VINHA, 2000).

6 FINAL CONSIDERATIONS

"To educate autonomy in children, therefore, it is useful to 'educate' them scientifically. But it is not enough to subject them to adult society and make them understand the reasons for their submission from the outside: autonomy is a power that can only be conquered from within and exercised in cooperation." Jean Piaget, 1932

The aim of this research was to hear what young people say about justice, a field that is still so obscure. The theoretical framework and the research contributed greatly to understanding the analysis of the speeches in the light of Piaget's proposal for cognitive development. This author places social experiences as a necessary condition for moral development, as well as the feelings they generate, the way they are elaborated and the role of authority figures, which are seen as fundamental for moral reasoning. This was, in fact, the core of this work.

The young people's answers about justice and injustice brought some surprises and confirmations. According to Piaget (1932/1994), cooperation plays an important role in moral development and the harmful effect that moral coercion has on intellectual development. The results of this study found that the absence of cooperation in the relationships maintained by young people promotes heteronomous talk about justice. The way in which the school and parents administer sanctions implies the construction of the notion of justice, although it was possible to observe contradictions in the young people's statements on the subject.

Some surprises emerged in relation to what young people think is fair in school practices in terms of their role in shaping students. Stereotypical statements that classify young people as alienated, disinterested and negligent with their cultural and ethical education are not in line with what was found in this study. In addition to plausible justifications about the role of the school, the group showed discernment about the importance of authority figures, especially the principal, in maintaining a fair school. In doing so, they revealed how great the school's difficulties are in dealing with fair sanctions. But is it the school that isn't prepared to meet the demands of these critical, daring young people, with their own singularities, but apparently without references in the adult model?

According to the participants, the school and all those involved face the problem of the many injustices that mark this scenario, starting with the principal's lack of dialog with the students. In resolving conflicts, managers seem to try to prove their authority through expiatory sanctions, such as suspensions and expulsions. Aren't these managers and teachers afraid of the new role expected of them in a democratic school?

In fact, implementing this new school requires building a social and moral environment which, in turn, requires solid knowledge about the intellectual and moral development of students. In the view of these young people, it's not the school that has lost its value, but the professionals who work in it who don't fulfill their role as educators. School should be a space for coexistence, and coexistence includes consensus, dissent and continuous negotiation, so that people learn to resolve conflicts, especially by giving up violence. In fact, for these young people, violence is not a form of justice, even though they agree with the application of punishments, especially when it comes to indiscipline. And if that's the case, they're asking for an interesting school, with different experiences from those they've had in their family environment, with clear and well-discussed rules, so that indiscipline no longer takes the place of learning.

On the other hand, a finding that unfortunately came as no surprise was the examples given by the young people of injustice - suffered or observed - which related to practices of racial and/or class discrimination. The young people's accounts also showed prejudice, which is to be expected when we understand that the causes of injustice are attributed or projected onto the white and financially well-off group. In the young people's opinion, they are the ones who should be punished. Injustice manifests itself notably through violence and it is this that justifies the speech that belittles, stereotypes and discriminates against those with greater economic power. They are responsible for the discrimination and violence that the police, for example, commit.

It is worrying to note that Piaget's studies on children's morality, carried out almost a century ago, have not yet had the desired repercussions on adults' relationships with children or young people, in other words, they still strengthen unilateral respect. For this author, reciprocal sanctions play an important role in establishing mutual respect, which is fundamental to the notion of justice, since this type of sanction takes into account both oneself and the other, establishing reciprocity.

During the research process, some observations became stronger in my view as an educator and mother. As long as conflicts are not seen as precious opportunities for individuals to self-regulate and as long as the school and the family do not deal with them fairly, based on mutual respect, there will hardly be any real opportunities for more ethical relationships. School rankings, the employee of the month and the medal for the best student are competitions that go against cooperation. In a society so marked by inequalities, so individualistic and so intolerant of differences, it would be opportune for institutions, especially schools, to mobilize themselves to reflect with students on ethical issues present in their daily lives.

In order to support those who want a more ethical society, it is important that academia also plays its part by helping school principals to take on a new role and meet this ethical demand, whether through research or extension projects. Studies into: the feelings and emotions that affect principals in their work, the difficulties they face in exercising democratic and cooperative management, the problems they encounter in mediating conflicts, would, for example, be very welcome. In the same way, it would be important to research and identify strategies that can replace expiatory sanctions with those that are reciprocal, something that is not achieved through classes, but through daily experience. In this sense, there should be room to deepen what is known about the role of student councils and school assemblies, to carry on discussions about what is right or wrong, and under what circumstances each one is, to promote the understanding that, when acting, it is necessary to put oneself in the other person's shoes and to discuss the need to abide by the rules, understanding their raison d'être and to rebel against them whenever they imply psychic or physical suffering for each and every individual.

Araujo, Puig and Arantes (2007) set out ten proposals for a values education project. Each of them would make a research project: the formation of the citizen; secular education and religious culture; and the time needed, the circumstances and the strategies involved in values orientation, so that the school can organize itself to give them during the periods when the students are at school. What is certain is that it is important to study how to build a moral culture at school, involving a new profile of educator who is willing to promote coexistence, participation and civic-mindedness, as well as dialog in conflict resolution.

The aspiration of this work was to study justice, but it was never thought that this would be enough. In fact, through it I have tried to glimpse the possibility of social change, of which parents and schools can be agents. I deeply hope that personal desires do not take precedence over justice, that the satisfaction of a pleasure does not come at the expense of anyone else. I hope that the indignation found in the young people's stories and the importance they attach to dialogue can echo far and wide, in the name of raising people's awareness of the most rational of virtues, which is justice. May the theory go beyond the shelves of books to become part of people's core values, governing their conduct.

BIBLIOGRAPHICAL REFERENCES

ARAUJO, U. F.; PUIG, J. M.; ARANTES, V. A. **Educagao e Valores:** Pontos e contrapontos. Sao Paulo: Summus, 2007.

ARISTOTLES. **Metaphysics:** Nicomachean Ethics. Sao Paulo: Victor Civita, 1984.

. **Rhetoric/Aristotle.** São Paulo: Colegao Folha, Grandes Nomes do Pensamento, 2015.

BATAGLIA, P. U. R.; MORAES, A. de; LEPRE, R. M. A. Kohlberg's Theory on the Development of Moral Reasoning and the Moral Judgment and Competence Assessment Instruments in use in Brazil. **Estudos de Psicologia,** Campinas, v. 1, n. 15, p. 25-32, 2010.

BIAGGIO, A. **Lawrence Kohlberg:** Ethics and moral education. Sao Paulo: Moderna, 2006.

BIBLIA. Portuguese. Holy Bible: containing the old and new testaments. Translated by Joao Ferreira de Almeida. Rio de Janeiro: Sociedade Biblica do Brasil, 1966.

BOCK, A. M. B.; FURTADO, O.; TEIXEIRA, M. de L. T. **Psicologias:** An introduction to the study of psychology. Sao Paulo: Saraiva, 2001.

BRAZIL. **Constitution (1988)**. Constitution of the Federative Republic of Brazil. Brasilia, DF: Senado Federal: Centro Grafico, 1988.

. **National Curriculum Parameters.** Transversal Themes. Brasilia: MEC/SEF, 1997.

CARR-GREGG, M.; SHALE, E. **Raising Adolescents.** Sao Paulo: Editora Fundamento, 2009.

CASASSUS, J. **Fundamentals of Emotional Education.** Brasilia - UNESCO: Liber Livro Editora, 2009.

COLBY, A.; KOHLBERG, L. **The Measurement of Moral Judgment.** Cambridge: Cambridge University Press, 1987.

COMTE-SPONVILLE, A. **Little Treatise on the Great Virtues.** Sao Paulo: Martins Fontes, 1999.

CORTELLA, M. S. **Qual e a tua obra:** Inquietagoes propositivas sobre gestao. Petropolis: Vozes, 2010.

CORTELLA, M. S.; LA TAILLE, Y. de. **In the Labyrinths of Morality.** Campinas: Papirus 7 Mares, 2013.

DEVRIES, R.; ZAN, B. **Etica na Educagao Infantil:** O ambiente socio-moral na escola. Porto Alegre: Artmed, 1998.

ELKIND, D. **Children and Adolescents:** Interpretive Essays on Jean Piaget. Rio de Janeiro: Zahar Editores, 1978.

FILHO, C. de B.; POMPEU, J. **A Filosofia Explica as Grandes Questoes da Humanidade.**

Sao Paulo: Casa do Saber, 2013.

GATTI, B. A. **Grupo Focal na Pesquisa em Ciencias Sociais e Humanas.** Brasilia: Liber Livro, 2012.

GILLIGAN, C. **A different voice.** Rio de Janeiro: Rosa dos Tempos, 1982.

GOERGEN, P. Moral Education Today: scenarios, perspectives and perplexities. **Educagao e Sociedade,** Campinas, v. 28, n. 100, p.737-762, Oct. 2007.

GONDIM, S. M. G. Focus Groups as a Qualitative Research Technique: Methodological Challenges. **Paideia**, Ribeirao Preto, v. 12, n. 24, p.149-161, 2003.

NATIONAL INSTITUTE FOR EDUCATIONAL STUDIES AND RESEARCH ANISIO TEIXEIRA. **Results.** Brasilia: Inep , 2012. Available at : <http://portal.inep.gov.br/internacional-novo-pisa-resultados>. Accessed on: February 20, 2016.

KANT, I. **Metaphysics of Customs.** Bauru: Edipro, 2003.

. **The Critique of Practical Reason.** Sao Paulo: Folha de Sao Paulo, 2015.

LA TAILLE, Y. de. **The Ethical Dimension in Piaget's Work.** 1993. Available at: <http://www.crmariocovas.sp.gov.br/dea_a.php?t=005>. Accessed on: Dec. 20, 2015.

. **Limits:** Three educational dimensions. Sao Paulo: Atica, 2000.

. **Morals and Ethics:** Intellectual and Affective Dimensions. Porto Alegre: Artmed, 2006.

. Morals and Ethics: a psychological reading. **Psicologia: Teoria e Pesquisa**, Brasilia, v. 26, p.105-114, 2010.

LA TAILLE, Y. de; KOHL, M.; DANTAS, H. **Piaget, Vygotsy, Wallon:** Psychogendic theories under discussion. Sao Paulo: Summus, 1992.

LIND, G. The Meaning and Measurement of Moral Competence Revisited: A Dual Aspect Model of Moral Competence. **Psicologia: Reflexao e Crftica**, Porto Alegre, v. 13, n. 3, p. 399-416, mar. 2000.

MAFFETTONE, S.; VECA, S. **The Idea of Justice from Plato to Rawls.** Sao Paulo: Martins Fontes, 2005.

United Nations Organization. **Universal Declaration of Human Rights.** Rio de Janeiro: UNIC, 2009.

PANIZZA, M. **Ensinar Matematica na Educagao Infantil e nas Série Iniciais:** Analise e propostas. Porto Alegre: Artmed, 2006.

PIAGET, J. **Psicologia e Pedagogia.** 3. ed. Rio de Janeiro: Forense Universitaria, 1975.

. **Where is Education going?** Rio De Janeiro: Livraria Josd Olympio Editora, 1977.

. **Moral Judgment in Children.** Sao Paulo: Summus, 1932/1994.

. **Representation in the World of Children:** With the help of eleven collaborators. Aparecida, SP: Ideias & Letras, 2005.

PIAGET, J. Las relaciones entre la inteligencia y la afectividad en el desarrollo mental del nino. In: DELAHANTY, G.; PERRES, J. (Orgs.). **Piaget and Psychoanalysis.** Mexico: Universidad Autonoma Metropolitana, 1952/1994.

RAWLS, J. **Justice and Democracy**. Sao Paulo: Martins Fontes, 2000.

RIQUE, J. et al. Moral Judgment of Young People in Different Political Contexts. **Arquivos Brasileiros de Psicologia**, Rio de Janeiro, v. 65, n. 2, p. 243-257, 2013.

ROSENBERG, M. B. **Nonviolent Communication:** Techniques for improving personal and professional relationships. Sao Paulo: Agora, 2006.

SANDEL, M. J. **Justiga:** What is doing the right thing? Rio de Janeiro/RJ: Civilizacao Brasileira, 2012.

TAVARES, M. R.; MENIN, M. S. de S. **Assessing Values in Schoolchildren and Their Teachers:** Proposal for the construction of a scale. Sao Paulo: FCC/DPE, 2015.

TIBA, I. **Quem Ama Educa!:** Forming ethical citizens. Sao Paulo: Integrare Editora, 2007.

TOGNETTA, L. R. P. **A Construgao da Solidariedade e a Educagao do Sentimento da Escola:** Uma proposta de trabalho com as virtudes numa visão construtivista. Campinas: Mercado de Letras, 2003.

. **The Formation of the Ethical Personality:** Strategies for working with affectivity at school. Campinas: Mercado de Letras, 2009.

TOGNETTA, L. R. P.; LA TAILLE, Y. de. The Formation of Ethical Personalities: Representations of Self and Morality. **Psicologia: Teoria e Pesquisa**, Brasilia, v. 24, n. 2, p.181-188, 2008.

VIDIGAL, S. M. P. **Formation of the Ethical Personality:** the contributions of Kohlberg and Van Hiele. 2011. 143 f. Dissertation (Master's in Education) - Faculty of Education, University of Sao Paulo, Sao Paulo, 2011.

VINHA, T. P. **The Educator and Children's Morality:** A constructivist view. Campinas: Mercado de Letras, 2000.

ANNEXES

ANNEX A - Critical Episodes Used in the Study

- Episode 1: The judge's dilemma

The secret service of a European country has evidence that a terrorist group is planning a bomb attack on a train that is often used during rush hour. The attack is scheduled for tomorrow. The terrorists intend to kill two hundred people and the group is known for its cruelty. The secret service has arrested a woman who is known to be one of the terrorist group's leaders. There is evidence that the woman took part in the attack plan. The police believe that they could prevent the attack if they could get her to talk. They interviewed the woman for several hours. However, she totally refuses to cooperate. The secret service fears that the woman won't talk before it's too late to prevent the attack. So they ask the judge in charge of the investigation for permission to torture her and force her to talk. In this country, torture is forbidden by law. Despite this, the judge gave permission to torture the woman in order to prevent the attack and save the lives of several people.

- Episode 2: The study

A 17-year-old girl is finishing high school and devotes most of her time away from school to studying, thinking about the ENEM exam. Her family is large, but she has her own room where she can study. However, a relative comes to live with them. This relative drinks and smokes and occupies the student's room, where she sleeps in the living room. Sleeping in the living room, she can't study and wakes up early because of the bright light, reducing her performance at school.

- Episode 3: Bikini photos

Two school friends have a bikini photo session with individual photos. One of the friends sends her photo to her friend's boyfriend, who finds out and physically assaults her at school. The principal witnesses the scene and suspends them both during exam time.

- Episode 4: The musician's son

To help with the household expenses, a 15-year-old son accompanies his father, who plays in bars at night. The son helps set up the equipment. The father usually drinks alcohol and is unable to drive again, so the son, who is underage, takes over the driving.

- Episode 5: Pop quiz

On a day of indiscipline in the 1st year of secondary school, the teacher threatens to tell them that the next day they will have a surprise test and that they will suffer for the mess they have made. One of the students, who was at school the other day to help out in the library, discovers that the test is on the coordinator's desk, goes there and manages to take a photo of the test and shares it with his class.

- Episode 6: Terminal illness

A woman has been ill for several years and after a long waiting list for tests, she discovers that she has a terminal illness and may not have long to live. After a few painful treatment sessions, she is waiting in hospital for a new dose of the medication that is essential if she is to stay alive, but the woman asks her daughter to take her home because she doesn't want to go through the treatment any more.

APENDICES

APPENDIX A - Informed Consent Form (minors)

Mr. Responsible/Legal Representative

I would like to ask for your permission for the minor to _______ participate as a volunteer in the research entitled: Justiga: vision of students seeking to improve their regular studies in a non-formal educational institution. This is a master's degree study at the Faculty of Education at PUC-SP, under the responsibility of researcher Edna Consuelo Leao.

The aim of this research is to hear what students say about the value of "justice", and the participation of young people will be of great importance in expanding knowledge on this subject in the field of moral psychology.

This research will involve a group of young people aged between 15 and 21. It will be a recorded and filmed conversation that will deal with everyday problem situations that involve thinking about what is fair or unfair, for 2 hours, in the very institution where they already study on Saturdays, after school, at 12 noon.

Research participants will not be subjected to any risk or discomfort and may leave at any time. Participation in the research will be free of charge.

The results will be analyzed and published, but the young person's identity and image will be kept strictly confidential. If at any time they do not wish to continue taking part, they can withdraw their consent at any stage of the research, without any harm to them.

For any information, you can contact the researcher by telephone: home (11) XXX or cell phone (11) XXX (operator XXX).

Post-Information Consent

I have been informed about what the researcher wants to do and why she needs the collaboration of ________________________________ , and I have understood the explanation. I therefore agree to take part in the project, knowing that I won't earn anything and that the young person authorized can leave whenever they want.

This document is issued in two copies, both of which will be signed by me and the researcher, with one copy remaining with each of us.

________________________________ Date: ____// ____
Participant's signature

____

Signature of the responsible researcher
RG

Thank you in advance for your cooperation.

APPENDIX B - Informed Consent Form (adult)

I invite you to participate as a volunteer in the research entitled: Justiga: the vision of students seeking to improve their regular studies in a non-formal educational institution. This is a master's degree study at the Faculty of Education of PUC-SP, under the responsibility of researcher Edna Consuelo Leao.

The aim of this research is to hear what students say about the value of "justice", and their participation will be of great importance in expanding knowledge on this subject in the field of moral psychology.

This research will involve a group of young people aged between 15 and 21. It will be a recorded and filmed conversation that will deal with everyday problem situations that involve thinking about what is fair or unfair, for 2 hours, in the very institution where they already study on Saturdays, after school, at 12 noon.

Research participants will not be subjected to any risk or discomfort and may leave at any time. Participation in the research will be free of charge.

The results will be analyzed and published, but your identity and image will be kept strictly confidential. If you withdraw your consent at any stage of the research, you may do so without any prejudice.

For any information, you can contact the researcher by telephone: home (11) XXX or cell phone (11) XXX (operator XXX).

Post-Information Consent

I have been informed about what the researcher wants to do and why she needs my collaboration and I have understood the explanation. I therefore agree to take part in the project, knowing that I will not earn anything and can leave whenever I want.

This document is issued in two copies, both of which will be signed by me and the researcher, with one copy remaining with each of us.

________________________________ Date: ____//____

Participant's signature

____

Signature of the responsible researcher
RG

Thank you in advance for your cooperation.

APPENDIX C - Informed Consent Form (Institution)

I, **Edna Consuelo Leao**, responsible for the research entitled: **Justiga: vision of students seeking to improve their regular studies in a non-formal educational institution**, master's student at the Faculty of Education at PUC-SP, hereby request authorization to carry out the research with young people from the Professional Initiation course at this institution.

The aim of this research is to hear what students say about the value of "justice", and the participation of young people will be of great importance in expanding knowledge on this subject in the field of moral psychology.

This research will involve a group of young people aged between 15 and 21. It will be a recorded and filmed conversation that will deal with everyday problem situations that involve thinking about what is fair or unfair, for 2 hours, in the very institution where they already study on Saturdays, after school, at 12 noon.

Research participants will not be subjected to any risk or discomfort and may leave at any time. Participation in the research will be free of charge.

The results will be analyzed and published, but the identification and image of the young people and the XXX Institution will be kept strictly confidential. If at any time you do not wish to continue taking part, you can withdraw your consent at any stage of the research, without any harm to you.

For any information, you can contact the researcher by telephone: home (11) XXX or cell phone (11) XXX (operator XXX).

Post-Information Consent

I have been informed about what the researcher wants to do and why she needs the institution's collaboration. That's why I agree to the institution taking part in the project, knowing that I won't earn anything and the young people allowed to leave whenever they want.

This document is issued in two copies, both of which will be signed by me and the researcher, with one copy remaining with each of us.

__________________________________ Date: ____//____
Signature of the person responsible for the institution
RG

____
Signature of the responsible researcher
RG

Thank you in advance for your cooperation.

Printed by Books on Demand GmbH, Norderstedt / Germany